The
Ceremonies
of the
Eucharist

Edited by Howard E. Galley

The Prayer Book Office

Morning and Evening Prayer

The Ceremonies of the Eucharist

A Guide to Celebration

Howard E. Galley

1989

COWLEY PUBLICATIONS
Cambridge, Massachusetts

Published in the United States of America by Cowley Publications, a division of the Society of St. John the Evangelist. No portion of this book may be reproduced, stored in or introduced into a retrieval system, or transmitted, in any form or by any means—including photocopying—without the prior written permission of Cowley Publications, except in the case of brief quotations embodied in critical articles and reviews.

Library of Congress Cataloging in Publication Data:
Galley, Howard E.
  The ceremonies of the Eucharist: a guide to celebration / Howard E. Galley
    p.   cm.
ISBN: 0-936384-83-2
1. Lord's Supper—Celebration. 2. Episcopal Church—Book of common prayer (1979). 3. Episcopal Church—Liturgy. 4. Anglican Communion—Liturgy. 5. Lord's Supper (Liturgy). 6. Lord's Supper—Episcopal Church. I. Title.
BX5949.C5G28   1989
264'.03036—dc20   89-22145

This book is printed on acid-free paper and was produced in the United States of America.

Fifth printing

Cowley Publications
28 Temple Place
Boston, Massachusetts 02111

For Robert and Albert

Cross references in this book refer to chapter and sections of chapters as listed in the Table of Contents. Thus (8) refers to the chapter on "Celebrations with Small Congregations," while 2.3 refers to the section "Of Deacons" in the chapter entitled "Of Liturgical Ministries."

Table of Contents

Cowley Publications is a work of the Society of St. John the Evangelist, a religious community for men in the Episcopal Church. The books we publish are a significant part of our ministry, together with the work of preaching, spiritual direction, and hospitality. Our aim is to provide books that will enrich readers' religious experience and challenge it with fresh approaches to contemporary issues in spirituality and theology.

Preface

Unlike liturgical manuals of the past, which were intended specifically for the use of the clergy, this book is directed to a wider audience—to members of parish worship committees, priests, organists and directors of music, lectors, deacons, cantors and other singers, bishops, altar guild members, acolytes—in short, to all who bear responsibility for the planning and conduct of public worship. In order to be as helpful as possible to such a variety of persons, the book includes, in addition to specific recommendations, the rationale and historical background for much of what is suggested.

The primary purpose of this book is to set forth a practical ceremonial usage for principal celebrations of the Holy Eucharist in medium-sized Episcopal churches. The needs of smaller and larger churches have also been taken into account, but the book is not intended as a complete customary for large cathedrals.

The directions and suggestions given in these pages assume a church with a free-standing altar and a presidential chair located behind it, such as is described in the first part of the book, "Of Churches and Their Furnishings" (1.1–1.2). Most of the directions are, however, fully appropriate, *mutatis mutandis*, to situations where the presidential chair is differently placed, and where the altar is located only a short distance from the wall, or even against it.

Page references to the eucharistic liturgy of the Book of Common Prayer are to the Rite Two Eucharist. Virtually all that is suggested is also applicable to Rite One, and the differences between the two rites are discussed in the section "Of Formularies Unique to Rite One" (3.9).

One of the extraordinary occurrences of the twentieth century has been the convergence of scholarly opinion, both Catholic and Protestant, about the classical "shape" or pattern of the eucharistic liturgy. For Anglicans, the name that springs most immediately to mind is that of the late Dom Gregory Dix, whose *The Shape of the Liturgy*, published in 1945, has had a profound influence on liturgical reform in most western churches. Today, whether one looks at the American Book of Common Prayer, the books of Alternative Services of other branches of the Anglican Communion, the *Roman Sacramentary* of Paul VI, the new *Lutheran Book of Worship*, or the revised service books of many other Protestant denominations, what one finds is essentially the same pattern:

> a. A liturgy of the word, typically including three Bible readings and a psalm, a sermon, and intercessory prayers.

> b. The eucharistic liturgy, consisting of the placing of bread and wine on the Lord's table, followed immediately by the offering of a prayer of thanksgiving over them; and a ritual breaking of the bread, followed by the administration of communion.

Such was, in fact, the ancient pattern. Later centuries added other elements, such as hymns and anthems, the Lord's Prayer and other prayers, the creed, and acts of penitence. Modern liturgies ordinarily retain these (though their placement in the service varies), but with one important difference: serious efforts have been made to keep the later elements from overwhelming the ancient core of the service or from interrupting it at points which obscure its basic pattern.

Scholarly studies have also focused on the ancient ceremonial of the eucharist. Of the earliest centuries, when Christian worship, being illegal, took place in private houses, we know but little. Our oldest clear evidence comes from the fourth century, when what had formerly taken place secretly was now being adapted to the more formal circumstances of public church buildings.

The ceremonial of the fourth and immediately following centuries was essentially functional. The basic purpose was to underscore the meaning of what was being done and said. It also provided for the orderly participation of many liturgical functionaries: acolytes, cantors, deacons, lectors, priests, etc. (a tradition which our 1979 Prayer Book has recovered). While impressive, it was far less complicated than what can be seen in many Episcopal churches today. It was also far more expressive than what can be seen in other Episcopal churches today.

The purpose of the present writer is not, it should be noted, to persuade Episcopalians into yet another "middle way," some being asked to simplify things and others to complicate them. Rather, the purpose is to help reintroduce Episcopalians to a part of our heritage. Our 1979 Prayer Book has given us a restored eucharistic rite which recaptures much that had been lost in the course of history. When, in the fourth and following centuries, that fuller rite was being developed, attractive and expressive ceremonial practices were developed to accompany it. Many of them are familiar to Episcopalians, but frequently in an attenuated or elaborated form that tends to blunt the original intent.

Practical experiments in the recovery of older practices began shortly after the Second World War. Some of these were done by Anglicans, both English and American. Some were done by Lutherans. Roman Catholic experiments, not surprisingly, were more controlled and seldom public. Increasingly, however, it became plain to all involved that many of the older ways helped to elucidate the meaning of the liturgy in ways that later practices did not. It was this discovery that prompted the revisers of the Roman Missal to return to the "noble simplicity" of earlier times when framing their ceremonial rubrics, and the present writer has happily taken advantage of the massive scholarship involved in their work.

It is, however, important to note that the rubrics of the Book of Common Prayer are not identical with those of the Roman Missal, and sometimes require or imply that different procedures be followed. A case in point is the placing of the bread and wine on the altar before the eucharistic prayer. The Roman rite has retained the late medieval practice of assigning this action to the priest-celebrant. Our Prayer Book (and the revised Canadian rite) has recovered the older practice of assigning this responsibility to the deacon. In every case, it is the Prayer Book rubrics that are here regarded as normative.

Detailed discussion of the rubrics will be found in the chapter "The Service in Detail" (5), which in some cases presents alternative suggestions, one of which may be more appropriate than the other in particular buildings. The chapter "Of Celebrations with Small Congregations" (8), though primarily concerned with early and weekday services, includes information which may also be helpful in planning principal celebrations in small churches and chapels. The "Synopsis of Ceremonies" (6) presents norms which, in the opinion of the author, are appropriate to most principal celebrations.

In the preparation of this book, I have been blessed with much useful help from others. Its faults or inadequacies, however, must be attributed to the author alone.

In particular, I would record my gratitude to Deacon Ormonde Plater for prompt, incisive, and persuasive criticism; to Mr. Mason Martens, who placed at my disposal his vast store of musical knowledge and lore; to Ms. Cynthia Shattuck of Cowley Publications for patient courtesy and sound advice; to the Rev. Walter L. Guettsche, the Rev. Thomas J. Talley, the Rev. Lloyd G. Patterson, and Mr. Frank L. Tedeschi, whose pertinent and helpful criticisms have made this a better book; and to Mr. Robert D. Gillespie, who typed the manuscript.

Howard E. Galley
Wednesday in Holy Week, 1989

1

Of Churches and Their Furnishings

1. Of the Place of Assembly

In the New Testament the word "church" is never used in reference to a building. "Church" refers to the Christian community, and especially to a body of the baptized gathered for worship. It is a body described in exalted terms—"a chosen race, a royal priesthood, a holy nation, God's own people" (1 Peter 2:9)—but it is not an assembly of likeminded persons. There are members who quarrel (Phil. 4:2), who promote factions (1 Cor. 11:18-22), and who hold differing opinions (Rom. 14:2-6). It is, moreover, a body that does not exist for its own sake, but is a people called by God to "make disciples of all nations" (Matt. 28:19), and to live in love and unity so "that the world may believe" (John 17:21).

The church is a body in which purely human distinctions of race, sex, and status are regarded as invalid (Gal. 3:28), but in which "all the members do not have the same function" (Rom. 12:4). Among the differing functions are those that pertain to bishops, presbyters, and deacons (Phil. 1:1; 1 Peter 5:1-3; 1 Tim. 3:1-13). All, however, are valued and valuable; they are "members one of another" (Eph. 4:25).

In the decades following the New Testament period, the distinction between ordained persons and other members of the church came to be expressed as "clergy and laity," and Christians eventually acquired buildings to worship in, but for centuries the greatest sense of privilege and honor continued to be attached to being part of the company of the baptized, and not to the company of the ordained.

This view of the dignity and importance of the laity did not, however, continue to prevail. With the passing of time—and for a variety of complex reasons—the laity came to be viewed as "clients" of the clergy, who no longer thought of themselves as celebrating services "with" the laity, but "for" them, and "dispensed" sacraments for their benefit. The space about the altar, where the clergy assembled, formerly referred to as the "presbytery," came to be called the "sanctuary," from which "mere" lay persons were ordinarily excluded. Their place was in the nave, which was clearly differentiated from the sanctuary.

It is interesting to note that this distinction finds no place in the historic rites for the dedication of a church. Nowhere is there a consecration of a "sanctuary" distinct from the nave. (Nor is there one in the rites of the present and former Books of Common Prayer.) The altar, to be sure, receives a separate consecration, but it is the walls of the church, and not some interior barrier, that defines the space set apart as sacred. What these rites evidently have as their purpose is the setting apart of a place of worship for the church as it understood itself in the early centuries, and as the 1979 Book of Common Prayer understands it: an assembly of the People of God in which the laity are as much a part of the celebration as the clergy. The place of the laity is therefore inside, rather than outside, the consecrated area.

Such an understanding of the function of a church building has obvious implications for the arrangement and furnishing of church interiors. Among them are:

a. The arranging of seating in a manner that fosters the sense of a community gathered.

b. The placing of the altar close enough to the people that it does not seem remote or isolated from them.

c. The placing of clergy seats in such a way that the priest can clearly be seen as one presiding at the assembly.

d. That aisles be wide enough to allow communicants to approach and return from the altar with ease, dignity, and reverence.

e. That if provision is made for communicants to receive the sacrament kneeling, the kneelers be obviously functional and not give the appearance of an architectural barrier between the altar and the people.

2. Of the Altar

A free-standing altar should be evidently free standing and not merely removed a few feet from the back wall, the effect of which can be to make the ministers appear to be standing behind a counter. At a minimum, there should be sufficient space to permit servers and other ministers to pass behind the priest and deacon with no appearance of crowding.

In planning new churches, and in remodeling old ones, care must be taken to ensure that the altar, while "feeling" close to the people, has sufficient space in front of it to accommodate a chair for the bishop and space for the candidates at baptism, confirmation, and ordination, as well as for the parties at weddings.

Anciently, Christian altars were not large and frequently only as wide as they were deep. (The long, shallow altar is a product of the period in which altars came to be placed against walls.) What is needed is a surface large enough for the sacred vessels, the altar book, and, if desired, a pair of candlesticks.

As the principal piece of furniture in the church, the altar should be truly beautiful. Whether of wood or of stone, it should be carefully designed and finely crafted. It should also look like a table.

In order that the ministers at the altar may be clearly seen by the people, a platform of sufficient height is a necessity. The platform, however, should not be so high that the ministers appear to be looking down at the people. Such steps as are needed should lead directly up to the platform. Additional steps in front of the altar itself should be avoided, since they inhibit easy movement around it.

3. Of the Credence

The credence is simply a convenient side table, and it is desirable that it not appear to be a major article of furniture. It should be large enough to accommodate comfortably all the vessels to be used in the celebration, together with the cruets and other things needful. Customarily, it is covered with a white cloth.

In a church where the eucharist is celebrated facing the congregation, the convenient place for the credence is on the "liturgical north" side of the chancel, that is, to the right of the priest and deacon as they face the people, and near where the deacon normally stands during the eucharistic prayer. A shelf underneath the credence may serve as a convenient place to put the alms basins after they have been removed from the altar, if there is not sufficient space on the credence itself.

4. Of the Lectern-Pulpit (Ambo)

Just as the attention of the people is focused on the altar during the celebration of the sacrament, so is it fitting that the reading and preaching of the word of God find its center in a single piece of furniture: a pulpit or lectern (ambo).

Ordinarily, the most convenient place for the ambo is to the right or left of the altar platform. It should be of a height which permits the reader or preacher to be clearly seen and heard, and should be easily accessible to lectors approaching it from the congregation, as well as to a deacon (or priest) bearing the gospel book and approaching it in procession from the altar.

Historically, the ambo is also the place from which the cantor (or lector) led the psalm after the first reading, and from which the deacon proclaimed the Exsultet at the Easter Vigil. It is also a suitable place from which to lead the prayers of the people.

5. Of the Presidential Chair

The traditional place for the presidential chair is directly behind the altar, but at some distance from it. The visual effect is to define the priest as one present to preside at a function in which all are participants, rather than as one present to act on their behalf or in their stead.

One objection sometimes heard is that the result is to place the priest too far away from the people. It must be remembered, however, that the chair does not remain a focus for very long. Very early in the service the focus of attention shifts, first to the ambo for the liturgy of the word, and then to the altar for the liturgy of the table.

In most situations it is necessary that the chair be raised on a small platform (two or three steps is generally sufficient) so that the priest can clearly be seen by all present. The chair itself should be of modest proportions and obviously functional.

6. Of the Font or Baptistry

The restoring of Holy Baptism to its proper dignity, as a rite performed in the context of public worship, implies that the font will be so placed that the congregation can both see and hear what takes place at it. Like the altar, the font should be truly beautiful, and the space about it sufficiently commodious to allow the ministers, candidates, and sponsors to gather at it without appearing to be crowded.

In some churches, the traditional placement of the font near the main entrance can be maintained. In others, some other location may be found to be better.

The font should be large enough to permit the immersion of infant candidates, and, when possible, should drain directly into the ground.

In building new churches and in remodeling old ones, serious consideration should be given to making provision for the baptism of adults by immersion or total affusion. Early Christian tradition, it may be noted, preferred baptism in "living," that is to say, "running," water, the water flowing from above into the baptismal pool. In modern installations this usually requires a mixture of both hot and cold water, in order that the baptismal water may be cool but not uncomfortably cold. A system of drainage is also necessary.

Such baptisms also require a place where the candidates can undress, and where they can dry off and be clothed after baptism. Clothes hangers, benches or chairs, mirrors, and a place for towels and combs will also be needed.

Near the font, or within the baptistry, a suitable table or large shelf should be provided, where the vessels and other things needed for the rite can be placed. The same area is also a suitable place for an aumbry where the sacred chrism can be kept between services. If desired, the oil for the anointing of the sick may be kept there as well, unless it is more convenient to keep one or both of them in the sacristy.

7. Of the Place of Reservation

The Prayer Book (p. 408) provides for the reservation of the consecrated sacrament, and the *Book of Occasional Services* provides a form for the dedication of an aumbry or tabernacle where the consecrated species may be "kept in safety."

As a place of safe keeping, it is important that the aumbry or tabernacle be either built in or securely fastened in place, and that it be provided with a good lock. (It is helpful to keep a duplicate key in the parish safe.)

For the reasons given later in this book, in chapter ten, entitled "Reservation of the Sacrament," it is desirable that the tabernacle or aumbry be large enough to accommodate two sets of vessels containing the sacrament.

It is important that the aumbry or tabernacle not dominate the place of worship. In the course of the liturgy, the presence of Christ is manifested in various ways: in the midst of the people gathered in Christ's name, in the reading and proclamation of the word, in the persons of those who minister in various ways, and finally, under the species of bread and wine. It is difficult for worshipers to experience and appreciate these various modes of presence if the place of reservation is so centrally located as to constantly call attention to itself, as is inevitable when a tabernacle is located on or behind the altar.

The following is therefore recommended:

a. When possible, the place of reservation should be in a separate chapel or room (or in a screened-off portion of a transept), attractively decorated, and conducive to private prayer and meditation. If the chapel contains an altar where weekday or early services take place, it is recommended that the aumbry be located in a side wall of the chancel. If the room or chapel does not contain an altar, an adequate credence should be provided, where the vessels containing the sacrament can be set down before being placed in the tabernacle or aumbry, and where necessary portions of it can be transferred from one vessel to another as needed.

b. When no other suitable place is available, it is recommended that the sacrament be reserved in an aumbry located in a side wall of the chancel of the church.

8. Of Lights

The first recorded use of lights in Christian worship occurs in the New Testament (Acts 20:8). There the use was obviously utilitarian, since the service was being held at night. By the third century at the latest, however, the bringing in or kindling of the evening lamp(s), whether at home or at a meeting of the church, was understood as a symbol of Christ, "the light [that] shines in the darkness" (John 1:5), and was frequently accompanied by a prayer of thanksgiving and/or a hymn. The Order of Worship for the Evening in the Prayer Book is a conscious revival of this practice, while the service of light at the Great Vigil of Easter is a special form of it.

Given this symbolic understanding, it is perhaps not surprising that the city churches built in the fourth century, after Christianity had been legalized, were supplied with sources of light for evening services that were far in excess of what was needed for adequate illumination. Lamps filled with olive oil (usually with floating wicks) were suspended before and above the altar, sometimes in clusters. Tall candlesticks, standing on the floor, were placed in the chancel and nave, and chandeliers bearing lamps or tapers illuminated the ceilings.

Lights were also used at the tombs of martyrs, many of which had churches built over them. Some of these were lamps that burned continuously; others were votive offerings of the faithful. This same honor was later extended to include pictures and images of saints.

No lights at all, however, were placed on the altar itself, which was considered too sacred to bear anything more than what was actually needed for the celebration of the eucharist.

The fourth century also witnessed the beginning of the practice of burning at least some of the lamps at the altar by day as well as by night—and not just at service time—a practice which is the basis of the tradition, which lasted for centuries, that at least one lamp should burn continuously in every church. (This tradition is still faithfully observed in many Lutheran churches, and should not be confused with the custom of burning a lamp before the reserved sacrament—a practice which was unknown before the thirteenth century.)

Such lavish displays of light were not, of course, possible everywhere, and especially not in the hundreds of small country churches built in the following centuries. For many, probably most of them, the single ever-burning lamp provided the norm. Additional lights, as needed and available, were used in service time, and on festivals extra lights were added.

None of the lights mentioned thus far, it should be noted, are specifically connected with the celebration of the eucharist. The only special use of light at that service was the practice of carrying candles at the reading of the gospel.

It was not until the eleventh century that candles were placed on the altar itself, a practice that was originally confined to the greatest festivals. These candles were lighted for the morning and evening services as well as the eucharist, and were removed at the end of the feast. This same period also saw a change in the shape of altars, from that of a cube to a shallow object as much as twelve feet long. Far more space was available than was needed for the vessels and altar book; and in many (though not all) churches, candlesticks, in varying numbers, gradually appeared to fill up the space. In larger churches, elaborate rules were devised, specifying the number of candles to be lighted on or about the altar on particular occasions.

Much of the polemic of the Protestant Reformers was directed against lights, especially those which burned before images and relics—practices which had, indeed, given rise to much superstition. The English Injunctions of 1547 demanded the removal of all lights except for "two upon the high altar, before the sacrament." Attempts to abolish these as well were thwarted by the death of King Edward and the accession of the Roman Catholic Queen Mary.

The reign of Elizabeth I saw the disappearance of candles from the altars of virtually all Anglican parish churches. The use of two, however, was carefully preserved in chapels royal, in most cathedrals and college chapels, and in the private chapels of bishops and lay nobles. In some places, at least, they were lighted at all services, not only at Holy Communion; and in other places (or during certain periods) were treated merely as decorations, and not lighted at all except when actually necessary.

The general recovery of the use of lights in Anglican churches occurred in the nineteenth century, which also introduced a distinction, unknown to history, between "eucharistic candles" (two candles placed on the altar itself and lighted only at celebrations of the eucharist) and "office lights" (the number of which sometimes suggested that Morning Prayer was more deserving of a great display of lights than the Holy Eucharist). The continuance of that distinction is not recommended.

As the preceding summary indicates, there has been no consistent tradition with regard to the use of candles.

The use recommended here, as a norm, is the burning of two candles at all services. These lights may be placed on the altar itself or on the floor at either end of it.

Alternatively, two torches may be used. These are carried in the entrance procession, placed in stands on the floor at either end of the altar, used at the gospel procession, and carried during the procession out. At services at which there are no servers to carry them, they are put in place before the rite begins.

If a larger number of candles is desired, torches may be used in addition to the two candles which burn on or near the altar.

In some places, processional candlesticks are used in place of torches. These are tall lightweight candlesticks, carried with one hand under the base and the other around the candlestick itself. When not being carried they are placed on the credence, or on the floor, or on a convenient shelf or shelves.

Where space permits, the use of additional lights on the principal feasts and in festal seasons is suitable. Such candles may be placed, for example, in standard candlesticks on the floor of the chancel, or in sconces on the walls. In some buildings, extra lights may also be placed in the nave. Such candle holders should not, however, be considered as fixed ornaments, and should be removed from the church in seasons when they will not be used.

Traditionally, candles used in church, and especially those on or about the altar, are made of beeswax. The Episcopal Church does not, however, have any rules on the subject, and other substances may be used as well.

In some churches, because of drafts, the use of "followers" on candles is a necessity. Metal ones, however, greatly diminish the beauty of candles by obscuring the glow that the flame casts into the top of the candles themselves. When needed, therefore, clear glass or plastic followers should be preferred.

Whenever possible, it is desirable that candles that are burning at the conclusion of a service remain lighted until the congregation has departed.

During the fifty days of Easter, the paschal candle is lighted for all services. The most suitable place for it is near the ambo. At other times it is appropriately placed near the font and lighted whenever baptism is administered. The Prayer Book also provides for its use at funerals (p. 467).

In planning new churches, and in remodeling old ones, it is suggested that consideration be given to recovering the practice of hanging lamps over or in front of the altar, either singly or in a cluster. Such lamps may be lighted for all regular services, or the use of some or all may be reserved for the more festal occasions.

The burning of a lamp before a picture or icon of the patron or some other saint or of the Virgin and Child (at least on occasion) is an attractive practice, and is not today likely to be the cause of superstition.

9. Of Crosses

It is desirable that there be only one cross visible in the chancel during the celebration of the liturgy. Depending on the architecture of the building and its furnishings, such a cross may be simple and unadorned, or elaborately decorated.

In a church with a free-standing altar, a fixed cross may appropriately be placed on the wall behind it, or it may be suspended over it. While it should be large enough to be seen, it should not be so large that it appears to lessen the importance of the altar itself.

When there is a cross above or behind the altar, the processional cross should be placed out of sight, or at least in a place where it is not facing the congregation, during the course of the liturgy.

An attractive alternative is to use the processional cross itself as the cross to be visible during the service, a practice which is very ancient. After being carried in the entrance procession, it is placed in a stand in a convenient place in the chancel, such as behind or beside the presidential chair; at the end of the service, the cross is carried in the procession out. Such a usage also makes possible some seasonal variety where that may be desired, an elaborate cross for days of special festivity and a simpler one at other times.

At services at which the cross is not carried, it is put in place before the rite begins. It may also be left in its stand outside of service time as a focus for private devotion.

The bearer of a processional cross holds the staff perfectly upright (not tilted forward), with one hand just below the cross and the other further down the staff, with the palms of both hands facing the bearer.

The custom of veiling the altar cross on Good Friday serves a practical purpose. By being concealed from view, it does not "compete" with the wooden cross brought in and placed in the sight of the people after the solemn collects (BCP p. 281). The practice of extending the veiling to the whole of Holy Week can be defended on devotional grounds; the congregation looks forward to seeing the cross unveiled. But the value of extending it back another week, which became the Roman practice (now merely allowed and not enjoined), or to the whole of Lent (which became the custom in northern Europe) is not apparent, and especially when it involves veiling crucifixes during the season in which they are most appropriate. The practice of extending the veiling is not recommended here.

10. Of Liturgical Books

The Prayer Book speaks of the lessons and gospel being read "from a book or books of appropriate size and dignity" (p. 406). The purpose of the rubric is to underscore the esteem in which the Scriptures are held in Christian tradition—which is less obvious when the lessons are read from a disposable printed sheet or a paperback book.

Whether the lessons which precede the gospel are to be read from a Bible or from a printed lectionary is a matter for local decision. The lectionary, however, has the advantage of identifying clearly who is speaking in the passage and, when necessary, provides the kind of introduction required by rubric (BCP p. 888). The result is to make the lector's task easier.

The use of a separate gospel book at principal services is specifically recommended.

The use of a bound altar book (or its loose-leaf equivalent) is recommended both for the liturgy of the word and the celebration of the sacrament.

The dignity of the altar is not enhanced when ministers and servers feel free to use it as a place to rest their prayer books, hymnals, and service leaflets. The only books that should be seen on the altar are the book of gospels, the altar book, and when needed, the *Book of Occasional Services*.

11. Of Vestments, Frontals, and Linens

The vestments worn at the eucharist are derived from the dress-up clothing of the late Roman Empire, the dominant culture of the world in which Christianity first took root. The only exception is the stole, which is a sign of office.

The basic garment is the alb, which is properly worn by all ministering at the service. Some albs are intended to be worn under other vestments, are put on over an amice (which is simply a neck cloth), and girded about the waist with a rope cincture. Other albs are designed to be seen, are more tailored in appearance, and frequently require the use of neither an amice nor a cincture. (In this book, when "alb" is mentioned, the use of an amice and cincture is assumed if the alb needs them.)

The surplice is a medieval variant of the alb. It is appropriately used as a substitute for it by all except the priest-celebrant, the concelebrating presbyters, and the ministering deacons.

The cotta is a shortened surplice. It is also far less attractive. Its use is not recommended, even for choristers and young servers.

Priests' stoles are worn over both shoulders, and hang straight down in front.

Deacons' stoles may be worn in three different ways:

a. Over the alb (and under the dalmatic), over the left shoulder, drawn across the chest and back, and fastened on the right side.

b. Over the alb (and dalmatic), with the center under the right arm, and the ends drawn across the chest and back and over the left shoulder to fall front and back.

c. Over the alb (and dalmatic), with the center on the left shoulder, and the ends hanging straight down front and back.

The chasuble is the distinctive vestment of bishops and priests at the eucharist. (It is also worn at the Good Friday and Holy Saturday liturgies.) Some modern chasubles are designed to have the stole worn over them. Most chasubles are not, however, and look best when worn over the stole. Chasubles worn at celebrations facing the people should be as attractive when seen from the front as from the back.

The dalmatic is the distinctive vestment of deacons, and its use is not confined to the eucharist. It may be worn at all celebrations, or only at the more festive times and occasions.

Chasubles and dalmatics, as pointed out above, began as articles of clothing, and it is desirable that they appear to be such. Their essential beauty should derive from their cut and choice of fabric, rather than from embroidery or other ornamentation. It is not necessary that the fabrics chosen should be "ecclesiastical"; decoration that suggests "slogans" should be avoided.

A cope may be worn by bishops and presbyters at services that do not include the eucharist.

The use of frontals to decorate the altar is very ancient. In their classic form they fall to the floor, sometimes on all four sides, sometimes only on the front and back. In the latter case the "fair linen" which covers the top of the altar falls to the floor at the ends.

The white altar cloth required by rubric at celebrations of the eucharist has historically been of linen. This, however, is no longer required, and other attractive fabrics may be used instead, including those that do not require ironing. Originally this cloth was identical with the corporal, covered only the top of the altar, and was put on during the offertory. The present rubric (BCP p. 406) is deliberately ambiguous, and permits, where it may be desired, a revival of the original practice. In most cases, however, the use of a corporal distinct from the altar cloth will be found more convenient.

The corporal is a square of linen (or other fabric) folded in such a way that, when refolded, it will trap within it any crumbs of bread that may have fallen on it during the breaking of bread, and which can then be conveniently consumed after the service.

The pall was originally a second corporal, kept folded, and used to protect the chalice from insects. When not needed, it should not be used.

Purificators are used to wipe the chalice. At large services, it is helpful if there are extra ones available at the credence.

The chalice veil is essentially an ornament. Though beautiful, its use is not necessary.

The burse is a case for corporals. Again, its use is not necessary.

Lavabo towels are used at the washing of the priest's hands. It is desirable that they be large enough to look like hand towels and not like napkins.

12. Of Vessels

Chalices are commonly made of precious metals, or at least plated with such metals. Other materials, such as glass or ceramic, are also suitable, provided they are not porous. As the most conspicuous of the sacred vessels, it is desirable that chalices be well designed and finely crafted. It is also important that they not be top-heavy.

Patens intended for wafer bread ("well" patens) are usually designed to fit on top of the chalice, which is a convenience when bringing the vessels to the altar at the offertory. Patens intended for leavened bread are, of necessity, considerably larger, as well as being deeper. They also may be made of any suitable material. It is desirable that the paten used be large enough to hold all the bread to be consecrated at the service. When necessary, additional patens can be brought to the altar at the time of the breaking of the bread and used in the distribution of communion.

Flagons are pitcher-like vessels, frequently with hinged covers, used to hold additional wine to be consecrated at the celebration. Like chalices, it is important that they be made of a non-porous material. In some places, the people's offering of wine is brought to the altar in a flagon, which is then used to fill the chalice. An attractive carafe or decanter may be used instead. When the amount of wine to be consecrated is small, a glass cruet of suitable size is commonly used.

Ciboria are chalice-like vessels, with covers, used to hold the consecrated bread. They are convenient vessels for holding the reserved sacrament but, because of their chalice-like appearance, are not recommended in this book for use during the liturgy.

Pyxes are small vessels, frequently shaped like pocket watches, used to take the consecrated bread to the absent. Ciboria are sometimes referred to as standing pyxes.

Bread boxes are small vessels, either round or square, with covers, used to hold wafers to be placed on the paten at the offertory. Such boxes may also be used, in place of a ciborium, for the reservation of the consecrated bread.

Cruets are used not only for wine, but for the water to be added to the chalice and for the washing of the priest's hands. It is helpful if the necks of the cruets are wide enough to make cleaning them easy. Stoppers are frequently easier to deal with than flanged metal covers.

Lavabo bowls are now generally the size of finger bowls. The original custom, however, was the washing of the priest's hands, not merely of the fingers. The earlier practice and the use of bowls large enough for this purpose is recommended here.

Patens and chalices used to communicate the sick and shut-ins are commonly smaller than those used in church. It may be questioned, however, whether they should be so small as to look like toys. The bottles for wine provided in many "private communion" sets, moreover, are difficult to fill and even more difficult to clean. In many cases, a small attractive bottle with a wide neck and a plastic-coated stopper will be found to be more practicable.

Ampullas are vessels designed to be poured from, used for the blessing and consecration of holy oils. They may also be used in administering such oils at public services. Between services, the oils are kept in tightly sealed bottles, labeled "Sacred Chrism," or "Oil of the Sick," as the case may be. Such oils may also be administered from "oil stocks," small cylindrical metal objects, packed with cotton, into which some of the oil has been poured.

Ewers are large pitchers with a wide spout used to fill the font at Holy Baptism, or to add to the water already present in the font.

Baptismal shells are commonly small, and made in the shape of sea shells. With the recovery of the tradition of using a significant amount of water, however, shells that are both larger and deeper are desirable. At the baptism of adults by total affusion, a large wide-mouth vessel with a handle will be found most convenient.

2

Of Liturgical Ministries

The liturgy is an action of the whole People of God. At it, all are participants; none are spectators. By virtue of their baptism, they share in the liturgy by right, each contributing to the whole.

The Holy Eucharist in particular provides the opportunity for the exercise of a wide variety of ministries. Some of these are ordained ministries. At parish celebrations, it is ordinarily a priest (rather than a bishop) who presides. There may be concelebrating presbyters (priests), who share in the celebration according to their order. Then there are the deacons, who function as servants of the church and heralds of the gospel.

Other ministries are lay ministries. One of these, assisting in the administration of communion, requires a license from the bishop; the others do not. There are the readers (lectors) who read the lessons that precede the gospel. There are those who (especially in the absence of a deacon) lead the prayers of the people. There are acolytes, who serve in a variety of ways. There are the cantor of the psalm and other singers, who lead the congregational singing and sing anthems. There are directors of music and instrumentalists. There are those who, in the name of the assembly, present the offerings of bread and wine at the altar. There are the ushers, who greet people, receive the money offerings, and assist in other ways. Finally, there are those "in the pews," who participate by joining in the responses, the prayers, and the songs; who offer to God of their substance; and who, together with the others, are nourished by Jesus Christ, present both in word and in sacrament.

At the root of these varied ministries lie different gifts and abilities, and although all the possible ministries may not be exercised at every celebration, the intent remains the same: to worship God and to build up the church in accordance with the gifts bestowed upon us. As the New Testament exhorts: "As each has received a gift, employ it for one another, as good stewards of God's varied grace" (1 Peter 4:10).

1. Of the Priest-Celebrant

Presbyters, by their ordination, are made pastors in the church of God. As such, and as representatives of the bishop, they preside at the celebration of the eucharist.

In the church's traditional understanding of the liturgy, the presiding function is regarded as a pastoral, as well as a priestly, act. While pastoral ministry does, of course, include a ministry to individuals, it also involves a ministry to the congregation as a whole. And it remains true that, for many people, the liturgy is the only occasion on which they come into regular serious contact with their pastor. It is, therefore, the priest's chief opportunity "to nourish Christ's people from the riches of his grace, and strengthen them to glorify God in this life and in the life to come" (BCP p. 531).

In the light of the responsibility involved, it seems only appropriate to affirm—since books on ceremonial sometimes seem to obscure the point—that far more is needed than a "correct" understanding of the ceremonies. The priest who presides well is one whose over-all comportment makes others comfortable, who listens attentively while others read, who proclaims the prayers with reverence and confidence, who preaches with conviction, and who avoids idiosyncracies that tend to distract others. No ceremonial guide can supply these. A well-ordered ceremonial can, however, enhance them and, in some particulars, help them to happen.

The term used in the rubrics to describe the person who presides at the liturgy is "celebrant." It is a term used for convenience, because it makes it possible to avoid saying "bishop or priest" again and again. It should not be understood, however, as implying that the presiding minister is the only celebrant. In the church's ancient understanding of the eucharist, all the baptized are celebrants, and all celebrate according to their order, whether bishops, priests, deacons, or lay persons. (In similar fashion, the church uses the term "priest" to describe one of the orders of the ordained ministry while, at the same time, insisting on the priesthood of all believers.) Since the concern of this book is with parish celebrations, the presiding minister is ordinarily referred to in these pages as "the priest."

In the course of the liturgy, the priest, as president of the assembly, performs the following functions:

a. Says the opening acclamation (and collect for purity).

b. Greets the people ("The Lord be with you") and says the collect of the day.

c. Blesses the deacon who is to read the gospel.

d. Ordinarily preaches the sermon.

e. May introduce the prayers of the people with a sentence of invitation.

f. Says the collect that concludes the prayers of the people.

g. Pronounces the absolution (when the confession of sin is used).

h. Introduces the exchange of the peace.

i. Proclaims the eucharistic prayer in the name of the assembly (using gestures appropriate to the particular prayer), and lifts up the paten during the doxology that concludes it.

j. Breaks the consecrated bread.

k. Says the invitation to communion (holding a portion of the bread over the paten), and administers the sacrament.

l. Leads the people in saying the postcommunion prayer.

m. Gives the blessing.

In the absence of a deacon (but when a concelebrating presbyter is present), the priest also:

a. Says the bidding to confession.

b. Holds up the chalice (as well as the paten) during the concluding doxology of the eucharistic prayer.

c. Holds the chalice (as well as the bread) during the invitation to communion.

d. Says the dismissal.

In the absence of both a deacon and a concelebrant, the priest also:

a. Reads the gospel.

b. Receives the gifts of the people, puts the bread and wine into the vessels, and places them on the corporal.

c. After communion, consumes the remaining bread and wine (assisted as necessary by others).

The traditional vestments of the priest are properly worn throughout the rite (including the sermon) in keeping with the historic custom of the church in both east and west. The practice, still sometimes seen, of not putting the chasuble on until the offertory, appears to be peculiar to Episcopalians. It dates, it seems, from the 1950s, the period in which eucharistic vestments were first introduced in many parishes. (To make the transition easier, some priests wore surplice and stole during the first part of the service and changed into eucharistic vestments at the offertory. At a later stage, an alb replaced the surplice.) It must also be pointed out that there is no precedent for wearing a cope (which is not a priestly vestment) during the first part of the service. The effect in both cases is the same: the liturgy of the word is seen as less important than the liturgy of the sacrament—and this at a time when liturgical renewal is concerned with recovering the balance of word and sacrament in a single unified liturgy. The traditional custom, as mentioned above, is to wear the same vestments throughout the service.

In the period following the Second Vatican Council, the Roman Church abandoned the use of the maniple and the custom of crossing the priest's stole, reforms which very quickly commended themselves to a number of Episcopalians and Lutherans. Since the effect is to bring western custom into closer conformity with the usage of the eastern churches, the adoption of these changes is recommended here.

2. Of Concelebrating Presbyters

The Prayer Book rubrics concerning what is commonly referred to as "concelebration" are not intended to suggest that it is inappropriate for priests to occupy places in the congregation and to receive communion along with the laity (p. 354). Their purpose is to provide a means whereby additional priests present in the chancel for any reason—such as to preach or to assist in the distribution of communion—may be given a share in the celebration appropriate to their distinctive order.

The most important occasions for concelebration are when the bishop is the principal celebrant, though the rubrics are careful not to restrict the practice to such occasions. A particular advantage of the practice is that it helps to manifest the presbyterate as a body, rather than as an aggregation of individuals.

The most obviously appropriate concelebrants at a parish liturgy are, of course, other priests on the parish staff. A visiting priest is another example. In a number of parishes, moreover, there are retired and non-parochial priests who are appropriately invited to participate in this way from time to time, and especially on occasions important to them, such as the anniversary of their ordination.

It is, however, important to remember that crowds of concelebrants are not appropriate in most parish churches. In a vast cathedral or immense church, the sight of a large number of vested ministers can be impressive; in most churches the effect is to make the chancel look overcrowded. It is also important that care be taken to ensure that the number of concelebrants is not disproportionate to the number of lay persons present. Under most circumstances, two concelebrants are the appropriate maximum on ordinary parish occasions.

The rubrics cited describe the concelebrating presbyters as appropriately joining "in the consecration of the gifts, in breaking the Bread, and in distributing Communion." There are two historical methods of joining in the consecration of the gifts:

a. By gesture only.

b. By gesture and by word (reciting part or all of the eucharistic prayer along with the priest in an undertone).

In this book, it is the first method, which is also the more ancient, that is recommended.

The tradition that concelebrating presbyters join in the breaking of the bread dates from a period in which a loaf (or loaves) of leavened bread were used, and where such assistance was manifestly helpful. Where large unleavened wafers are used, the ceremony can still be carried out, although in most cases the assistance of only one of the concelebrants will be sufficient.

As many of the concelebrating presbyters as are needed assist in the distribution of communion.

In the present Roman rite, the concelebrants communicate themselves, a practice derived from present-day Byzantine usage. However, this was not the ancient custom. Originally, the priest communicated the concelebrants, but only after first receiving communion at the hands of one of them. It is this practice that is recommended in these pages.

Should there be, for good reasons, a large number of concelebrants, it is important that the communion of the people not be delayed. In such cases, the priest, having communicated a few of the concelebrants and the deacon, should proceed to communicate the people, leaving two of the concelebrants to communicate the rest of them and then join in the administration to the people.

The concelebrating presbyters participate in the liturgy as follows:

a. They vest in alb and stole, and, if possible and desired, chasuble.

b. At the entrance procession they walk immediately ahead of the priest (and deacon, if the deacon walks beside the priest).

c. They (may kiss the altar if the priest is to do so and) go to their assigned seats. They do not, however, displace the deacon or deacons, who sit at the priest's right and left.

d. Just before the eucharistic prayer (or, if incense is used, immediately before or after being censed), they take their places about the altar in such a manner as not to be in the way of the deacon or deacons. It is also important that they not obstruct the view of the congregation. If there are only one or two of them, as recommended, they may suitably stand at either end of the altar.

e. During the eucharistic prayer, they participate in one of the following ways:

    1. They stand with hands joined, except during the invocation of the Holy Spirit, when they extend both hands, palms down, toward the bread and wine. (They may also extend their right hands at the words "This is my body…" and "This is my blood….")

    2. Alternatively, they:

    —Stand with hands joined during the introductory dialogue.

—Stand with hands extended during the preface.

—Join their hands (and bow if the priest does so) at the Sanctus; then stand with hands extended whenever the priest does so, and with hands joined at other times.

—At the words "This is my body..." and "This is my blood...," extend their right hands toward the gifts.

—At the invocation of the Holy Spirit, extend both hands, palms down, toward the bread and wine.

f. After the prayer they bow low, even if the priest genuflects.

g. As needed, they assist in the breaking of the bread.

h. After the invitation to communion, one of them communicates the priest and is communicated in turn. The rest of them then receive communion (standing), and then either assist in communicating the people or return to their seats.

i. They depart in procession in the same order in which they entered. (They do not kiss the altar before departing.)

In the absence of a deacon, one or two of them also perform the diaconal functions listed in section 4 below.

3. Of Deacons

The ministry of deacons is a servant ministry. By their ordination they are set apart to show forth, and to help others to show forth, the redemptive love of him who came "not to be served but to serve" (Mark 10:45).

The liturgical functions of deacons are a direct reflection of their ministry in the world as heralds of the gospel and servants of all, particularly those in need.

In the course of the liturgy the deacon ordinarily performs the following functions:

a. Carries the gospel book at the entrance procession. (If not carrying the book, walks beside the priest.)

b. Proclaims the liturgical gospel (and sometimes preaches).

c. Leads the prayers of the people.

d. Says the bidding to confession and leads the confession.

e. Brings the vessels to the altar at the offertory, spreads the corporal, receives the gifts of the people, puts the bread and wine into the vessels, and places them on the corporal.

f. If incense is used, censes the ministers and people at the offertory (unless it is preferred that the thurifer do so).

g. Removes the money offerings from the altar and takes them to the credence.

h. Lifts up the chalice at the doxology that concludes the eucharistic prayer.

i. Brings any needed additional chalices and patens to the altar at the time of the breaking of the bread. Fills the chalices and, if needed, assists in the bread-breaking.

j. Holds the chalice during the invitation to communion.

k. In the absence of a concelebrating presbyter, says the words of administration quietly to the priest at the time of the priest's communion.

l. Administers the wine or, if necessary, the bread.

m. Consumes the remaining bread and wine (assisted as necessary by others), then takes the vessels to the credence and either cleanses or covers them.

n. Says the dismissal.

o. Walks beside the priest during the procession out.

Formerly, in addition to performing these functions, the deacon served as a master of ceremonies, a practice that it is desirable to restore. From the deacon's traditional place at the priest's right, the deacon is in the perfect position to observe all that goes on, to judge how many people are present, and therefore to know how much bread and wine will be needed and how many additional vessels may be required. Also, to give any needed cues to the servers and, if something goes wrong, quietly to set it right. By accepting the responsibility of overseeing the "mechanics" of the service, the deacon makes it possible for the priest to preside with less distraction, and consequently with greater attentiveness, to the function of presiding.

When not otherwise occupied, the deacon's usual place during the liturgy is at the priest's right, both at the chair and at the altar. When at the altar, the deacon normally stands a few steps back, so as to allow the priest to pray with hands widely extended.

A second deacon, when present, occupies the seat at the priest's left. In such cases, the diaconal duties are shared. During the eucharistic prayer, the second deacon stands near the altar, but not at the priest's left in places where it is customary for the acolyte to turn the pages in the sacramentary.

The deacon's traditional vestments, alb with stole and dalmatic, are appropriately worn by all deacons present. When necessary or when preferred, however, the dalmatic may be omitted.

4. Of a Priest Acting as Deacon

The restoration in recent decades of the diaconate as a life-time vocation and ministry raises questions about the wisdom and appropriateness of priests vesting as, and acting as, deacons. While it cannot be said that the practice is forbidden by the rubrics of the Prayer Book, it must also be said that they do not encourage it. (What the rubrics do say, BCP p. 354, is that in the absence of a deacon an assisting priest may perform certain diaconal functions.)

It would be more faithful to the rubrics as a whole if, in places where there are two priests and no deacon (which is typical of many parishes), the assisting priest functioned as a concelebrating presbyter and that the functions of the deacon be divided among the other ministers.

When this practice is adopted, the assistant priest vests as a priest, in alb and stole (with chasuble), and performs the functions proper to a concelebrant as described above.

The diaconal duties are apportioned as follows:

a. The concelebrant or a vested reader bears the gospel book at the entrance procession. Alternatively, the book may be placed on the altar before the service begins.

b. The concelebrant reads the gospel.

c. A lay member of the congregation, or a cantor, leads the prayers of the people.

d. The priest says the bidding to confession.

e. The (adult) acolyte brings the vessels to the altar and spreads the corporal.

f. The concelebrant receives the gifts of the people, puts the bread and wine into the vessels, and places them on the corporal.

g. The thurifer censes the ministers and people at the offertory.

h. The priest lifts up the chalice, as well as the paten, at the doxology to the eucharistic prayer.

i. The concelebrant brings any needed additional chalices and patens to the altar at the breaking of the bread, fills the chalices (and assists in breaking the bread).

j. The priest holds the chalice, as well as the bread, during the invitation to communion.

k. The concelebrant (after communicating the priest and being communicated in turn) assists in communicating the people.

l. The concelebrant consumes the remaining bread and wine (assisted by others as necessary), then takes the vessels to the credence and cleanses or covers them.

m. The priest says the dismissal.

5. Of Lectors

The office of reader, or lector, is among the oldest, if not the oldest, of liturgical lay ministries.

In the early church, lectors were frequently appointed on a permanent basis. They were selected on the evidence of their ability to read well, and it was expected that they show forth in their lives the truth of the lessons they read. The normal expectation was that one or more lectors would exercise their ministry at every celebration of the eucharist. In the middle ages, however, the office declined in importance as, increasingly, it became customary for the lessons to be read by persons in "major orders."

The present Prayer Book has restored this ancient function to the laity, but not as a permanent office. According to the rubric (p. 354), the reader or readers are to be "appointed by the celebrant." In actual practice, however, readers are frequently assigned on a rota basis, and this is clearly the better way, since it gives them opportunity to study and rehearse the passages to be read. (It is important to distinguish the persons so appointed from "licensed lay readers," whose historic liturgical function is to officiate at the daily offices rather than to read lessons.)

The traditional functions of lectors are:

a. To read the lessons which precede the gospel.

b. To lead the psalm that follows the first reading (when it is not sung by a cantor or choir).

It is also appropriate (especially in the absence of a deacon) for lectors to lead the prayers of the people.

It is of vital importance that the readings be clearly heard, and that those assigned to read them have the ability to project their voices in such a manner as to make this possible. The well-trained lector will also be aware that:

a. While eye contact with the congregation is important before beginning the reading, so that the reader can be assured that the people are comfortably seated and ready to listen, it is not at all necessary, and frequently distracting, during the reading itself.

b. A "dramatic" reading of the text is not appropriate, because it focuses the people's attention on the lector rather than on what is being read.

c. Congregations lose their ability to follow if the lesson is being read too fast.

d. A distinct pause needs to be made between the end of the reading and the acclamation "The Word of the Lord."

e. It is frequently helpful for the lector to "lead" the silence which follows the lesson by remaining at the reading stand, either with eyes closed or fixed on the book.

f. If the psalm which follows the first reading is to be led by the lector, the lector should also be the one to announce it and give the page number (if necessary), and should wait until the people have found their places before beginning it.

g. If the gospel is to be read from the same lectern or pulpit, and from a gospel book, the reader of the lesson which precedes the gospel must remember to remove the lectionary from the reading stand before returning to place.

There is no necessity to restrict the ministry of lector to adults. Teenagers who read well should also be encouraged to serve in this capacity.

The traditional vesture of readers is the alb or surplice. In many places, however, the lectors do not vest, and occupy seats in the congregation. Both practices have advantages.

In the absence of a deacon, a vested lector may carry the gospel book at the entrance procession. In such cases, the lector walks immediately ahead of the priest (or priests), puts the book on the altar, and then goes to his or her seat.

In order to underscore the dignity and importance of the ministry of lector, it is desirable (when possible) that those assigned to read at a particular celebration not function as acolytes or ministers of communion at the same service.

6. Of Cantors and Choirs

Among the many happy results of liturgical renewal is the rediscovery of the usefulness of the ministry of cantors.

The original function of the cantor in Christian liturgy was to sing the psalms between the lessons. In some places, apparently, the psalm was sung straight through as a solo. The classical method, however, was to sing it responsorially, and it is this method which is generally favored by liturgists today. In this method, the congregation participates by repeating a refrain after the cantor, and after each verse, or group of verses, of the psalm.

Since the psalm is an integral part of the liturgy of the word, it is desirable that it be sung from the same lectern or pulpit at which the preceding lesson was read.

In places where an alleluia or tract is used before the gospel, it is sung by the cantor from some other convenient place, so as not to be in the way of the gospel procession.

Cantors can also lead the congregation in singing other parts of the service and, when there is no choir, can make a sung service a viable possibility. For suggestions in this regard, see *The Hymnal 1982*, Accompaniment Edition, Volume 1 (Service Music), pages 11-12.

Choirs perform two functions at the eucharist: they fulfill their own proper liturgy by singing anthems and, sometimes, other music; and they lead the congregational singing.

It is important that choirs be placed where they can best be heard. In many churches a rear gallery, or a raised platform at the back of the church, is the best choice. In others, especially when the building is almost square, a position in the nave near (but not in, or in front of) the chancel is best.

The usual vesture of choirs is cassock and surplice. If in a gallery, however, the choir need not be vested.

Prior to the mid-nineteenth century, choirs were ordinarily in place before the service began, and a recovery of this practice is highly desirable for musical reasons. The following directions include suggestions for doing this in a convenient way.

The members of the choir:

a. Immediately before the prelude, go in single file—without any cross, banner, or other emblem—to their places by the shortest convenient route.

b. On arrival, they kneel or stand (according to individual preference) to offer their private prayers, and then sit for the prelude.

c. Except when fulfilling their own proper liturgy (for which they ordinarily stand), they stand, sit, and kneel like other members of the congregation, join audibly in the responses, and behave as exemplary worshipers.

d. They receive communion after other members of the congregation or toward the end of the distribution.

e. At the end of the service they depart in single file, either during the exit of the ministers from the chancel, or during the departure of the people.

For directions about liturgical processions before the eucharist, see 3.10 below.

7. Of Lay Eucharistic Ministers

The administration of communion by lay persons at the celebration of the eucharist does not represent a recovery of ancient practice; it is a concession to the pastoral needs of the present time. While the early church had no hesitancy about the propriety of lay persons—even children when necessary—taking communion to the shut-in and imprisoned, the administration of the sacrament during the service was regarded as one of the duties of the ordained in their ministry to the People of God. In keeping with this tradition, the Prayer Book (p. 408) and the canons (Title III, Canon 3) specify that only in the absence of a sufficient number of priests and deacons are lay persons to fulfill this ministry. It is important, however, that this legislation be interpreted generously. In many congregations the administration of communion still takes far too long. In most situations it is best if there are two persons with cups for each person ministering the bread.

It will be noted that in this book, expressions like "chalice bearers" are not used to describe these lay persons, since they do not just "bear" such vessels. They are true ministers of communion.

The exercise of this ministry requires a license from the bishop, which may be granted for any period of time up to three years. In some parishes, and in some dioceses, those who have been licensed for a specified time are required to wait a year or more before being licensed again. The purpose, of course, is to give others an opportunity to fulfill this function.

The proper vesture of lay eucharistic ministers is an alb or surplice, and it is desirable that they be vested.

The right of communicants to say "Amen" before receiving the sacramental species is an ancient one, and is frequently referred to in the writings of the church fathers. It is important, therefore, that ministers of the chalice complete the words of administration before raising the cup to the communicant's lips. Persons carrying vessels containing the consecrated sacrament do not reverence the altar or the cross—or anything else.

8. Of Acolytes

Acolytes first appear in Christian history as assistants to the deacons in their regular duties of distributing alms, visiting shut-ins and prisoners, taking communion to the absent, and generally ministering to those in need. Their liturgical duties, which may have begun somewhat later, are analogous: they "serve" during the celebration of the liturgy.

From the beginning, and for centuries afterward, the liturgical ministry of acolytes was an adult ministry. Today, in contrast, it is largely a ministry of children and adolescents.

It is no part of the purpose of this writer to disparage or discourage the ministry of youngsters at the altar of God. What is questioned is the tendency to restrict the ministry of acolyte to them alone. In an era in which great emphasis is laid on lay ministry in and to the world, it would seem only appropriate that lay adults be frequently seen in a corresponding ministry as acolytes in the assembly of the faithful.

The ceremonial directions in this book therefore specifically provide for the participation of one adult acolyte at every principal celebration, and assign to that person a number of the ancient functions of that office. It would be fitting for a lay eucharistic minister to fulfill this function, at least from time to time.

In the course of the liturgy, this acolyte appropriately performs the following duties:

a. Carries the processional cross in the entrance procession.

b. Holds the sacramentary (altar book) before the priest whenever the priest is to read from it, from the beginning of the service until the exchange of the peace.

c. Assists the deacon (or priest) at the receiving of the people's offerings.

d. Places the sacramentary on the altar for the eucharistic prayer (and, where it is customary, turns the pages for the priest).

e. If needed and licensed, assists in administering communion.

f. After communion, assists as needed in taking the vessels to the credence. Folds the corporal and takes it to the credence.

g. Puts the sacramentary in place, or holds it, for the postcommunion prayer.

h. Carries the cross in the procession out.

In the absence of a deacon, the acolyte also:

a. Brings the vessels to the altar at the offertory and spreads the corporal.

b. Removes the money offerings from the altar before the eucharistic prayer.

c. After communion (and the consuming of the remaining bread and wine), takes the vessels to the credence and either cleanses or covers them.

In the absence of both a deacon and an assisting (concelebrating) priest, the acolyte also brings any needed additional vessels to the altar at the time of the breaking of the bread.

Directions for the candlebearers (torchbearers) and the thurifer will be found in 1.8, 3.8, and in chapters 5 and 6.

9. Of Masters of Ceremonies

On occasions when the ceremonies to be performed are complex, such as during Holy Week and at ordinations, it is frequently helpful to appoint a master of ceremonies. Such a person is properly regarded as a special assistant to the deacon.

The most suitable person to exercise this ministry is usually an experienced adult acolyte who is intimately acquainted with the details of the service, and who has the ability to handle complex matters in an inconspicuous manner.

The use of a master of ceremonies at ordinary parish celebrations is neither necessary nor recommended.

10. Of Subdeacons

The office of subdeacon appears to have come into being in a manner similar to that of acolyte. In a number, though by no means all, of ancient dioceses, the number of deacons was long restricted to seven (see Acts 6:1-6). When such dioceses were large, as in the case of the diocese of Rome, the subdiaconate formed the means of providing additional diaconal services such as poor relief and the administration of diocesan institutions.

With the passage of time, subdeacons were assigned various duties at the altar (especially at large diocesan services), and eventually supplanted the lectors as the ordinary readers of the liturgical epistle. They also finally acquired a distinctive vestment, the tunicle, modeled on the deacon's dalmatic.

Of particular importance, however, is the fact that, in the tenth century, the subdiaconate came to be regarded in the western church as the "lowest" of the three "major orders" of ministers. In this view, the three orders of the apostolic ministry were subdeacons, deacons, and priests (bishops being regarded as priests to whom certain particularly important functions were reserved). The medieval solemn mass, therefore, in which the priest is "assisted" by a deacon and subdeacon, was believed to show forth the ordained ministry in its fullness.

In reaction to this view, and to assert unequivocally that the three orders of the apostolic ministry are bishops, priests, and deacons, the English reformers abolished the subdiaconate completely. In 1972, in the wake of the Second Vatican Council, the Roman Church did the same thing—and for the same reason.

In the light of this history, it may well be questioned whether the functioning of persons referred to as "subdeacons" is of help to Episcopalians in their understanding of the Church's ministry and liturgy. It is, of course, realized that in some parishes the practice is of long standing, and that pastoral prudence may dictate that it not be terminated abruptly.

Where this is the case, it is recommended that the "subdeacon" fulfill the functions assigned in this book to the adult acolyte, but should not (except when actually necessary) read any of the lessons. It is further recommended that the use of the tunicle be abandoned or at least restricted to the principal feasts or the festal seasons and occasions.

11. Of Ushers

Ushers are the modern equivalent of the ancient office of doorkeeper. Normally, they greet people upon arrival and provide them with leaflets or books as may be necessary. In crowded churches they appropriately help people to find seats. In most places they also (1) deal with late-comers, (2) receive and present the money offerings, and (3) direct the people on their way to the altar to receive communion.

a. The seating of late-comers should be done tactfully and as inconspicuously as possible. It is best done during the singing of hymns or other chants. To the extent possible, it should not be done during prayers, or during the readings and the silences which follow them. The well-trained usher will politely indicate to late-comers that they should wait at the back of the congregation and, as soon as it is appropriate, invite them, or help them, to find a seat.

b. Since practice varies from congregation to congregation, it is important that ushers know precisely when to bring the money offerings to the altar. When possible, it is best that this be done by only one of the ushers. Whether it is ushers or other members of the congregation who bring forward the bread and wine is a matter of parish practice. Ordinarily, the presenters of the bread and wine walk directly behind the usher who carries the money offerings.

c. The Prayer Book (p. 407) contains a rubric which specifies that the priest is to receive communion "while the people are coming forward." The ushers, therefore, must be ready to direct the first of the communicants to approach the altar immediately after the invitation to communion, "The Gifts of God for the People of God."

The approach of the people is properly understood as a kind of procession: those in the front of the church going forward first, followed by those in the seats behind them in a steady stream. It is far better that there should be many people waiting in the aisle than to create the impression that the communicants are approaching in "groups" or "blocks" of individuals. In many churches a single usher in the center aisle is all that is needed.

Especially at this solemn point in the liturgy, it is important that ushers remember that theirs is a pastoral and helping function; attitudes appropriate to traffic control (though admittedly a temptation) are to be avoided.

The task of the ushers is usually easier if the choir receives communion after the congregation. At times, however, it may be necessary for the ushers to interrupt the communion procession for long enough to allow the choir to join in it at an earlier point. Ushers commonly, though not necessarily, are the last to receive communion.

In some churches, it is necessary to station at least one usher at the door throughout the service to guard against individuals seeking to enter and cause a disturbance. It is desirable that such ushers be instructed in methods of dealing with such persons firmly and gently.

12. Of the Congregation

In Anglican churches, as in the early church, the baptized take an active part in the liturgy. To them belong responses, songs, hymns, and other formularies; and by their "Amens" they ratify, and make their own, prayers spoken by others. In addition, they:

a. Reverence the altar with a deep bow before taking their seats. If the sacrament is reserved in the chancel, they may genuflect instead.

b. Kneel or stand for private prayer.

c. Stand at the entrance of the ministers.

d. Make the sign of the cross at the opening acclamation, and remain standing until after the collect of the day.

e. If there is a sprinkling of the congregation, make the sign of the cross when sprinkled.

f. Sit for the reading of the lessons and the singing or reading of the psalm.

g. Stand for the sequence hymn and/or alleluia or tract.

h. Stand and face the reader during the reading of the gospel. Make the sign of the cross with the right thumb on the forehead, lips, and breast when it is announced.

i. Sit for the sermon.

j. During the administration of Holy Baptism, face the font for the parts of the rite that take place there.

k. Stand for the creed, bow the head at the mention of the name of Jesus, and bow low at "By the power . . . and was made man."

l. Stand for the prayers of the people.

m. Kneel or bow low for the confession of sin. Make the sign of the cross at the absolution.

n. Stand and exchange the peace with those about them.

o. Stand and join in the offertory hymn if one is sung. Otherwise sit until the offerings are brought forward.

p. If incense is used, bow before and after being censed.

q. Stand for the eucharistic prayer. At individual option, may kneel after the Sanctus, but stand again for the Lord's Prayer.

r. Reverence the sacrament (a genuflection or low bow) before going forward to receive it.

s. Receive the bread in the palm of the right hand, with the left hand supporting it, and respond "Amen" before eating it. Respond "Amen" before drinking from the chalice. Guide the chalice to the lips with both hands.

t. After returning to place, kneel or stand for private prayer, then sit.

u. Stand and join in the postcommunion hymn, if one is sung.

v. Stand for the remainder of the service. Make the sign of the cross at the blessing if one is pronounced. In Lent, if a prayer over the people is said, kneel or bow low, then stand for the dismissal.

w. After the dismissal and departure of the ministers, may offer a brief private prayer before departing. A better place for such prayers, however, is immediately after communion.

x. Reverence the altar before leaving the church, or, if the sacrament is reserved, may genuflect.

3

Of Seasons, Music, and Liturgical Practices

1. Of Feasts and Seasons

The Prayer Book designates seven days in the year as "principal feasts" (p. 15). Five of these are integral parts of the two great festal periods in the church year: (1) the great fifty days from Easter Day through the Day of Pentecost, which very early in Christian history came to be observed as a time of continuous rejoicing, and (2) the similar festal period of the nativity cycle, extending from Christmas Day through the First Sunday after the Epiphany (the Baptism of our Lord).

By their very nature, these festal periods are the proper times for the use of the best vestments, the finest frontals, and the most elaborate music. They are also the appropriate times for the use of additional candles, flowers, and other decorations.

The same degree of festivity is also appropriate on the two principal feasts which fall outside these seasons, Trinity Sunday and All Saints, and on the local feasts of the patron or title of the church and the anniversary of its dedication.

Each of the two great festal periods is preceded by a season of preparation. Lent, the season of preparation for Easter, is a time of penitence, fasting, almsgiving, prayer, and study, which finds its proper climax in the celebration of Holy Baptism and the renewal of baptismal vows at Easter. Characteristic of the Lenten liturgy is the omission of Gloria in excelsis, the suppression of the use of Alleluia, and the reading of Scripture lessons chosen to illustrate the great themes of the season.

During Lent, it is desirable that the church itself reflect the austerity of the season. Where there is a mural or picture behind the altar (and it is not a representation of the crucifixion),it is appropriately concealed from view by a veil of a color that does not call attention to itself. Banners and other decorations (including pictures) are appropriately removed and the use of flowers avoided. Ornate candlesticks are suitably replaced by simpler ones, and the use of a special processional cross is appropriate. Medieval Lenten processional crosses were generally of wood, stained or painted a deep red, and usually were not crucifixes.

Traditionally, the fourth Sunday in Lent, commonly referred to as Refreshment Sunday, has been an exception to the usual Lenten austerity. On this Sunday flowers may be used, and, if the church possesses two sets of vestments of the appropriate color, the more elaborate set is suitable.

Advent, the season of preparation for Christmas, has a character very different from that of Lent. It is not a penitential season or a time of fasting. Essentially, it is a time of joyful expectation, and it is this theme which predominates in the appointed lessons. A rich frontal and elaborate vestments are fully appropriate, as is the use of other decorations. The principal liturgical change is the suppression of Gloria in excelsis, which gives the entrance rite a more subdued character. Alleluia, however, is not suppressed, and occurs very frequently in the hymns and anthems proper to this season.

The remaining Sundays of the year (except for the second and last after Epiphany and the last after Pentecost) do not have a distinct seasonal character. Liturgically, these "green" Sundays are characterized by the semi-continuous reading of the New Testament (i.e., the passages are read in the same order in which they occur in Scripture). What these Sundays celebrate is Sunday itself—the Lord's Day, the basic and essential Christian feast—on which God is glorified for his work in creation, in raising from the dead our Lord Jesus Christ, and in bestowing on his church the gifts of the Holy Spirit.

In addition to the principal feasts and Sundays, the Prayer Book lists a number of other feasts of our Lord, together with other major feasts, which are to be observed in the course of the year (pp. 16-17). Three of these (Holy Name, Presentation, and Transfiguration), when they occur on Sunday, take precedence over the Sunday; the remainder are normally transferred to a weekday. The rubrics do permit, however, that when such a feast falls on a "green" Sunday, it may displace the Sunday service. It is suggested that advantage be taken of this rubric only in the case of feasts of our Lord and on the feasts of SS. Peter and Paul, St. Mary the Virgin, St. Michael and All Angels, and the patronal feast.

2. Of Liturgical Colors

The use of liturgical colors to mark the seasons and holy days of the church year is a late medieval development of the western church. By the time of the Reformation, a considerable number of variable color schemes were in use, and the normal expectation was that parish churches would (to the extent possible) follow the usage of the cathedral. In some places, notably in France, diocesan color schemes continued to be used as late as the eighteenth century.

The English reformers, however, unlike the Lutherans, disapproved of such practices and abolished them. No system of liturgical colors was in use in Anglican churches until the nineteenth century, when interest in such matters was once again kindled. The color scheme then adopted in most parishes (especially in the United States) was the now familiar white-red-violet-green sequence "borrowed" from contemporary Roman Catholicism.

Despite its widespread use and general acceptance, its suitability to Anglican churches is occasionally questioned, usually on two grounds: (1) that it is Roman and not the scheme that was in use in England before the Reformation, and (2) that it does not adequately distinguish between the seasons of Advent and Lent.

The first objection seems to rest on a misunderstanding. There was no single use of liturgical colors in pre-Reformation England. As elsewhere in Europe, usage varied from diocese to diocese. But that does not mean that the white-red-violet-green sequence was unknown there. It was, in fact, in all essentials the usage of the dioceses of Canterbury, London, and Exeter, which would appear to be ample precedent for its use by modern Episcopalians. With regard to the second, it can only be said that the sharing of a liturgical color does not make two seasons alike. Christmas and Easter are very different seasons—yet the color for both is white. There is, moreover, nothing to prevent a parish from having two sets of violet vestments, an elaborate set for use in Advent and a very simple set for Lent. (In some churches, a variant of violet—rose—is used on the third Sunday of Advent and the fourth Sunday in Lent.)

The principal argument for the use of the white-red-violet-green sequence today, however, is not its origin but the fact that it has become an ecumenical usage. As the most widely-used scheme in Anglicanism, the official scheme of the Roman rite, and the ordinary use of the Lutheran churches, it can rightly be seen as a treasure the liturgical churches hold in common. It is, therefore, the use recommended in this book.

Particular attention is called to one variation from the scheme. In recent decades there has been a revival of the ancient use of red (crimson or scarlet) for Holy Week among both Episcopalians and Lutherans. The Roman rite has restored the use of red only on Palm Sunday and Good Friday. The use of red throughout the week is recommended here.

Other variants, in use in some places, are the practices of using royal blue in Advent and unbleached linen (Lenten array) in Lent. This was the custom in the diocese of Salisbury (Sarum) and a number of other northern European dioceses. The practice is, of course, fully legitimate, but it cannot claim to be an ecumenical usage. In this book, therefore, as noted below, these colors are recommended for frontals, rather than for vestments.

The use of a fixed color scheme for vestments does not, of course, mean that the altar frontal must be of the same color; when the usual position of the ministers is behind the altar, it sometimes looks better if it is not.

Many free-standing altars look good without a frontal and, when this is the case, it would be appropriate to use one only at selected times. A simple and attractive use is to have only one frontal—a "festal" (gold or multi-colored) frontal, designed to harmonize with both red and white vestments. Such a frontal would appropriately be used throughout the two festal periods and on the other festal days described in the previous section.

A predominantly blue frontal is appropriate for Advent and complements nicely many violet vestments.

A Lenten frontal, if used, should reflect the austerity of the season. In many places, an unadorned frontal of unbleached linen or fabric of a similar color and texture can give the altar a look of great simplicity.

Pulpit falls, if used at all, need not be of the color of the vestments.

3. Of Saying and Singing

Discussions of the choral service tend to focus on how much, if any, of the priest's and deacon's parts are to be sung. A more important question is why parts of the service which, by their very nature, are songs, such as the Gloria in excelsis and the Sanctus, are so frequently said instead of sung. One even encounters celebrations attended by hundreds of worshipers, at which there are four or more metrical hymns and one or more anthems sung by a trained choir, at which these two texts are merely recited.

It is therefore important to point out that it is fully legitimate to sing these two songs, or at least the Sanctus, even at celebrations at which there is no other music whatever. (It is also appropriate to sing the Sursum corda dialogue and the preface in such circumstances.) *The Hymnal 1982*, it should be noted, deliberately includes settings of the Sanctus (S121, S122, and S123) and of the Gloria (S272, S273, and S274) which are intended to be sung by congregations without instrumental accompaniment. Similar settings of Kyrie eleison (both in Greek and English), of Christ our Passover, Agnus Dei, and other fraction anthems are also provided.

Another part of the service that by nature is a song is the appointed psalm. If a responsorial setting is used, this can frequently be sung even when the congregation is quite small. All that is needed is a competent cantor (who, if necessary, can be the lector) and two or three persons with enough confidence to "lead" the others in singing the refrains. If the psalm cannot be sung, it should be recited rather than omitted.

The alleluia, tract, or verse before the gospel is also a song, but it is essentially a musical acclamation. If it cannot be sung it should not be used.

Whether—and how often—the priest's and deacon's parts should be sung, and whether the lessons and/or gospel should be chanted, are not matters of principle. Practice varies greatly, and the variety of practice is fully legitimate. The concern here is that the parts of the service that are songs be sung as frequently as possible.

The singing of the whole service is, of course, the ancient tradition—a tradition probably derived from the practice of the synagogue. Though frequently alleged, there is no evidence that it had anything to do with making the service easier to hear. Since chant was understood as a form of elevated speech, it was regarded as particularly suitable for the worship of God.

Music is available for all the appointed texts of the eucharist except the confession of sin and the postcommunion prayer. (The latter could be sung by all on one note.)

The singing of hymns and anthems, though eminently desirable, is not essential to the sung service. Accordingly, even at weekday services at which there is no choir or instrumentalist, a fully sung service is more frequently a possibility than is commonly supposed.

4. Of the Music of the Ordinary

The term "ordinary" is used to describe the fixed texts of the eucharist, as opposed to those that are "proper," like the collect, lessons, and psalm, which change from celebration to celebration. In the Latin liturgy which is the ancestor of our Prayer Book rite, four of the texts of the ordinary are songs: Kyrie eleison, Gloria in excelsis, Sanctus (including Benedictus qui venit) and Agnus Dei. The Nicene Creed has frequently been accounted a part of this group.

Originally, these were all songs of the people, and usually only one setting was in use. This does not mean, of course, that only one setting of each existed, but that in a given region only one was commonly used.

When Latin stopped being the universal (or widely understood secondary) language of the west, the singing of these pieces became the responsibility of choirs. From this time, roughly the ninth century, the number of settings began to grow. In some cases, alternatives were in use—an elaborate setting for festal occasions, and a simpler one for other times. Sometimes, settings were assigned on a seasonal basis, or as appropriate to particular groups of holy days, such as feasts of apostles. In a period when the mass was sung daily in many cathedral and monastic churches, this musical variety helped maintain the interest of singers in these unchanging texts—interest which might otherwise have focused exclusively on the elaborate music of the proper anthems: introit, gradual, alleluia or tract, offertory, and communion.

By about 1450 it had become customary for composers to treat the five musical texts of the ordinary as a set, musically unified and intended to be used together, and referred to as "masses." This began a tradition which was to find its most elaborate expression in the great Viennese masses with orchestra of the 18th and 19th centuries. In those masses the series of texts is treated in manner similar to movements of a classical symphony.

There is no doubt that treating the texts as a set has provided us with some of the most precious musical jewels of western civilization. It has also provided us with widely-used congregational settings. One thinks immediately of Healy Willan's *Missa de Sancta Maria Magdalena* (the "Second Communion Service" in *The Hymnal 1940*). It is also a tradition that is still very much alive. But it is neither a liturgical nor an artistic necessity.

No one demands that the hymns used at a given celebration should all be sung to music written by one individual and published on the same date. Yet the situation is, in fact, the same. Like hymn texts, the texts of the ordinary are the product of different times and places. They are not an intentional set.

A rigid insistence that they be treated as such comes at a high price. To refuse to use an attractive Agnus Dei because the Gloria and Sanctus that "belong" with it are judged too difficult (or too dull) is to limit one's available repertory. The same is true when one declines to use a Haydn Gloria in excelsis on a great feast because parish policy requires a congregational Sanctus. If one feels a need to "balance" things, an offertory or communion anthem or motet by a composer of the same school is an attractive possibility.

It is the realization that the texts of the ordinary are individual hymnic texts, and that settings of them can stand on their own, that persuaded the editors of *The Hymnal 1982* to abandon the experiment of *The Hymnal 1940* of printing "complete" communion service settings. Instead, as was the practice in earlier hymnals, all the settings of Kyrie eleison are grouped together, as are, for example, those of the Sanctus and Agnus Dei.

A word also needs to be said about "plainsong masses." These are, in fact, compilations. A single setting of each of the texts of the ordinary, drawn from various sources and composed in different centuries, but deemed by a music editor to belong together, are published as a unit, and given a name. A familiar example is the *Missa Marialis* (the "Fourth Communion Service" in *The Hymnal 1940*). Another is the *Missa Dominicalis.* The same practice can be seen in the numbered masses in the Roman Kyriale of 1905, which uses all the pieces in the two masses just mentioned, but in different groupings. The contents of such masses should be seen for what they really are: individual pieces available for use ad libitum.

It is sometimes asserted that Episcopal congregations are required to limit their repertory of music for the ordinary to settings included in the official hymnal. Such an assertion fails to take into account the fact that the only part of the hymnal that is set forth by authority is the *words*. The Episcopal Church does not legislate in the matter of musical settings. Clergy and musicians, working together, are free to make such use of the settings in the hymnal (whether of hymns or of the texts of the ordinary) as are appropriate to particular congregations; and to select, compose, or commission such other settings as may be desired.

For recommendations about settings of the song texts of the ordinary, see the discussion of each piece in "The Service in Detail" (5.A.8, 5.A.9, 5.C.12, 5.C.18). For the creed, see 5.B.8.

5. Of Instrumental Music

The organ, as "king of instruments," has long enjoyed a place of preeminence in the worship of the church. The use of other instruments, including the piano, is also suitable.

In general, a real organ is to be preferred to an electronic instrument. In most churches the organ need not be large. What is important is that it be so placed that it can be heard to its best effect—not placed in an alcove or so heavily encased that its sound is muffled.

The rubrics provide that "on occasion, and as appropriate, instrumental music may be substituted for a hymn or anthem" (BCP p. 14). The practice is not infrequent at the offertory and during communion, though it is obviously not intended to be the norm—note the words "on occasion."

The use of instrumental music in place of an entrance hymn or chant is rare, but it is an available option. At the bishop's visitation, especially if the full ceremonial described elsewhere in this book is used, the use of instrumental music makes it possible for all to watch the procession. If desired, the instrumental piece could be followed by a brief hymn, begun as the bishop enters the chancel.

Preludes and postludes are not dealt with by the rubrics, though their use is common and, in many places, expected. There is much to be said in favor of well-selected preludes. They can prepare the congregation to worship better by helping them to relax and free their minds of petty distractions. They can prompt devotion, or be occasions of simple enjoyment.

There is, unfortunately, still a lingering suspicion in the minds of some musicians and clergy that preludes should be, at most, mezzo forte, while postludes should be loud. There is, of course, no basis for this supposition, and anyone who has experienced the thrill of hearing a truly grand (even bombastic) piece being played at the beginning of a festal service knows how wrong the supposition is.

Postludes are a very different matter. In most places they are not listened to, despite the hours of practice devoted to them. They simply "cover" the departure of the worshipers, which was, in fact, their historic purpose. If, on the other hand, as happens in some places, people (apart from the liturgical ministers) are encouraged to remain until the postlude is over, then the dismissal is not being taken seriously. The same argument applies here as applies to a "final" hymn (see 5.C.29).

In most situations a short piece, begun immediately after the dismissal, long enough to cover the exit of the liturgical ministers—but no longer than that—is all that is needed.

The practice of playing "bridges" between stanzas of hymns needs to be regarded with caution. There may, indeed, be occasions when a hymn needs to be "stretched." In most places this will happen only on days when the liturgy begins with a festal procession. In these circumstances, the bridges serve also to give the singers a rest. When done for mere effect, however, or to exhibit the skill of the musician, the practice is intrusive and quickly becomes tedious. This is especially true in the case of hymns sung at the offertory.

The use of other instruments, either in addition to or in place of the organ, is rare in Episcopal churches (apart from occasional "guitar masses"). Even in small congregations, however, there are sometimes highly competent instrumentalists, and it is suggested that they be invited to play during services from time to time.

6. Of the Posture for Prayer, Bowings, and Genuflections

The early Christians knew of two postures for prayer, standing and kneeling, both of which are attested in the New Testament (Mark 11:25, Acts 9:40). Both references are to private prayer, but both practices became characteristic of public worship as well.

As the tradition developed, kneeling became associated primarily with private devotion. In public worship its chief association was with days of fasting and penitence, and church councils expressly forbade the practice on Sundays and during the fifty days of Easter.

For those who had been "raised with Christ" (Col. 3:1) and made "a kingdom of priests" (Rev. 5:10), the usual posture for public prayer was standing. Particularly was this so for the eucharistic prayer (which in form is essentially a thanksgiving) and for the prayers of intercession, which were regarded as part of the people's priestly ministry of reconciliation.

Similarly, as members of a priestly people, all stood to receive communion.

The present Prayer Book has sought to recover the older tradition, while at the same time showing pastoral sensitivity to those habituated to the western medieval tradition of kneeling, characteristic of previous Books of Common Prayer. Thus, no posture is specified for the prayers of the people, and while all must stand for the first part of the eucharistic prayer, individuals who desire to do so (which should not include those in the chancel) may kneel after the Sanctus.

The practice suggested here is to kneel only for the confession of sin (except for those behind the altar) and absolution. It is also suggested that those who kneel after the Sanctus be encouraged to stand for the Lord's Prayer.

Bowing the head at the mention of the name of Jesus is a custom that survived the Protestant Reformation, and it is required in the English Canons Ecclesiastical of 1603. In actual practice, however, it came to be restricted to its mention in the creeds. This book specifies it in that context (5.B.8); its use at other times is also appropriate.

A bow of the head is also appropriate:

a. When the three divine Persons are mentioned together, as in the Gloria Patri.

b. At the dismissal of those who have brought up the alms and oblations.

c. By priest and server after the washing of the priest's hands.

Bowing to the altar is also a custom that survived in some places, despite Puritan opposition. It was commended by the English Canons of 1640, and has once again become common practice. The canons spoke of this reverence as being made only twice in the course of the service: on arrival before the altar at the beginning, and before departing at the end. This was the ancient custom, is the practice of the new Roman Missal, and the practice recommended in this book. This reverence, it should be noted, is made to the altar itself, and not to the altar cross (if there is one).

Originally, this reverence was a deep bow from the waist, and a recovery of that tradition is desirable.

A deep bow is also traditional before and after being censed and at certain other times within the liturgy. See the Synopsis of Ceremonies (6.).

Historically, the genuflection is a variant of the deep bow, but it has come to be associated exclusively with the consecrated sacrament. A genuflection by the priest at the conclusion of the eucharistic prayer is recommended in chapter 5. When the sacrament is reserved in the chancel, a genuflection (toward the altar) may be substituted for the profound bow at the beginning and end of the service. No reverence is made to an aumbry or tabernacle during the liturgy.

It is important to remember that practices such as kneeling and standing, bowing and genuflecting, are intended as aids to devotion. Persons who by reason of infirmity find them difficult or painful should be encouraged to feel free to omit them.

Persons carrying objects to be used in the liturgy do not bow or genuflect.

7. Of Stylized Gestures and Procedures

The reason for recommending the adoption of certain "stylized" gestures and procedures is not to stifle individuality. Rather, the purposes are:

a. To make certain actions sufficiently automatic that the person doing them is freed to give attention to primary matters, including the needs of others.

b. To avoid idiosyncrasies that tend to distract or annoy other people.

c. To help ordinary people appear less awkward.

d. To avoid accidents.

Some traditional gestures and practices are derived from the customs of the cultures in which Christianity first took root; some are the result of the historic experience of the Christian community; some are more or less arbitrary; some are simply practical common sense.

The following practices are specifically recommended:

a. One never backs down steps. Even when only one step is involved, one turns completely around and moves forward.

b. When going from one place to another—except when a deliberate ceremonial movement is involved—one goes by the shortest route, unless by doing so one would appear to be discourteous.

c. When kneeling, one kneels on one knee first. When rising, one begins with the other foot. The effect is to minimize the chance of getting one's foot caught in the skirt of the cassock or alb.

d. When standing, kneeling, or bowing, if the hands are not otherwise occupied, one joins them before the breast, rather than letting them hang down at the sides or holding them clasped before the groin. There are three ways of holding the hands joined:

—With fingers lightly intertwined.

—With one hand over the other.

—With palms pressed together and the right thumb over the left.

e. When making a gesture with one hand, one holds the other flat against the breast.

f. When genuflecting, the body is kept perfectly upright (not bent forward), and the hands are joined. One then touches the ground with the right knee at the place where the foot was, and rises at once. When standing at the altar, however, one places the hands, palms down, on the altar when genuflecting.

g. When bowing the head, the neck is bent, but the shoulders are not hunched forward. The movement is made slowly, so as not to suggest a mere bobbing of the head.

h. When making a deep or profound bow, one bends the body from the waist and bows low enough that it would be possible to place a hand on one's kneecap. The movement is not hurried.

i. When sitting, one does not slouch or cross the knees or ankles. Except when holding a book or leaflet, the hands are placed in the lap or on the knees.

j. When making the sign of the cross upon oneself, the left hand is placed flat against the body below the breast. With fingers held together, one touches the forehead, breast, left shoulder, and right shoulder with the right hand.

k. When making the sign of the cross over the congregation, the same parameters are observed. In other words, it is the size of the person making it that determines the size of the cross. The fingers are held together, facing up, palm flat and to the left. If standing at the altar, the left hand may be placed on it.

l. When making the sign of the cross over the bread and wine, the fingers are held together, pointing forward, palm facing to the left. Both lines of the cross are traced in a horizontal plane, a few inches higher than the tallest vessel.

m. When extending the hands over the bread and wine in blessing, one holds them palms downward, fingers pointing forward, thumbs almost touching, a few inches above the tallest vessel.

n. When greeting the people with the words "The Lord be with you" and at the greeting of peace, one looks at them, and extends the hands, palms up, at full arm's length, toward them.

o. When praying with hands extended—the classic "orans" position—the arms are extended outward and upward. In the course of history, this position was severely modified: the arms were lowered so that the elbows touched the body and the palms were facing each other. The recovery of the more expressive ancient practice is recommended.

p. When praying collects, one extends the hands for the body of the prayer, but joins them at the beginning of the conclusion (usually, but not always, at "through Jesus Christ our Lord") and keeps them joined until the end. The one who says the collect does not, of course, join in the "Amen."

q. When bringing the chalice to the altar, one does not place it in the center, but to the right of it, so that it does not have to be moved when the corporal is spread.

r. When spreading the corporal, one places it, still folded, on the altar, a little further back than necessary, with the exposed hem to the right. One then unfolds it in the following order: left, right, back, front (exactly the opposite of the way it was painstakingly folded); then, grasping the two front corners, draws it forward to the edge of the altar. If, after unfolding, one notices that it had been improperly folded, and is upside down, one does not turn it over, since it will then not fold up properly at the end of the service. If it is backwards, with the cross toward the back, one either leaves it alone or folds it up again before turning it around.

s. When filling chalices, and when using a pall to cover or uncover a chalice, one either holds the chalice with the other hand or places the other hand firmly on the foot of it. The purpose, of course, is to guard against upsetting it.

t. When putting a pall on the chalice, one places it with the smooth (unembroidered) side down. After taking one off, one places it on the altar with the smooth side up. The reason is to prevent any wine stains on the pall from being transferred to the altar cloth.

u. When holding a chalice with both hands—as the priest does at the words of institution and the deacon does at the conclusion of the eucharistic prayer and the invitation to communion—one grasps it below the bowl with one hand and places the other beneath the foot of it.

v. When ministering the chalice, it is wise not to let go of it, but to allow the communicants to guide it to their lips and drink from it. This is more easily accomplished if the communicants are reminded, from time to time, to follow this practice. When communion is received standing, the procedure is virtually a necessity, since in many cases the minister cannot see into the cup.

w. When kissing the altar (a traditional gesture of respect), one stands back from it a little, places the hands flat on it, and bends straight down to touch the table with the lips. When kissing the gospel book, one lifts it to a comfortable height, and kisses the beginning of the text just read. The kissing is done noiselessly.

x. When holding the sacramentary (altar book) for the priest to read from, one holds it facing away from oneself, and at a height convenient for the particular priest.

y. When turning pages for the priest at the altar, or when pointing to a text on the page, one does so with the left hand. The purpose is to avoid jostling the priest.

8. Of the Use of Incense

The early Christians made no liturgical use of incense. So identified was the practice with pagan religion and, in particular, with the cult of the Roman Emperor, that the only use of it they were prepared to accept was metaphorical. See, for example, Revelation 8:3-4, where it symbolizes the prayers of the saints.

With the establishment of Christianity as the religion of the empire, and the decline of paganism, attitudes began to change and various ceremonial uses of incense were introduced. In the western church, the primary uses were honorific and festal, with incense carried in processions of the clergy and of the gospel book. At a later period, the practices of censing the gospel book, oblations, altar, cross, and people were introduced.

Incense is appropriate at any celebration of the eucharist:

a. At the entrance of the ministers, after which the priest may cense the altar.

b. At the gospel.

c. At the offertory.

Using incense at any one of these three points does not necessitate its use at the others. Both the size of the building and pastoral prudence should be taken into account. Where the use is infrequent, it may be wise to use it only at the gospel or at the offertory. Where incense is regularly used, it is suggested that it be used at both these points on most occasions, its use at the entrance being reserved to the principal feasts and festal seasons.

Handling a thurible is not something one can easily learn from books. Instruction by an experienced thurifer is virtually a necessity. The basic actions may be summarized as follows:

a. The thurifer hands the boat to the deacon (or the priest if there is no deacon).

b. The thurifer holds the censer, open, and at a convenient height, before the priest. This is done by grasping the chains just above the cover, the end of the chains being held in the other hand.

c. The priest spoons incense into the censer and, if desired, blesses it by making the sign of the cross over it, saying nothing.

d. The thurifer closes the censer and holds it with one hand; then receives the boat back with the other hand. (At the gospel the deacon or priest hands the boat to the acolyte or a server, who takes it to the credence.)

At the censing itself, the person who is to do the censing holds the censer with the left hand, then grasps the chains, just above the bowl, with the right hand, and swings it forward, away from the body.

At the censing of the altar, the priest walks around it, counterclockwise, swinging the censer continually.

At the offertory, if there is a cross behind or above the altar, the priest may cense it in the course of censing the altar. Having come to the middle of the front of the altar, the priest stops, raises the censer high, censes the cross with three swings, and then completes the censing of the altar. If the cross is located elsewhere, such as beside the altar, the priest may cense it when passing in front of it.

At the gospel, the deacon or priest censes the book with three swings: first in the center, then to the left, then to the right.

The censing of the oblations is done in the same way—with three swings. (In some places a more elaborate method is used. The priest first makes three signs of the cross with the censer over the oblations, then circles the vessels with the censer three times, the first circle being made clockwise and the other two counterclockwise. A variant of this practice uses only one cross and one circle.)

In medieval usage, the censing of the ministers and people became a highly complicated procedure, performed in descending hierarchical order, the principal ministers being censed individually and with differing numbers of swings. Post-Reformation Roman usage complicated it even further by distinguishing between double and simple swings. The laity were censed collectively with single swings.

The present Roman Missal has abolished the distinction between kinds of swings, and simply speaks of censing the priest and people.

The recommendation made here is to cense all present collectively, using single or double swings as may be convenient, but without regard to rank or seniority.

The deacon or thurifer:

a. Censes those in the chancel with three swings, bowing to them before and after doing so.

b. Proceeds to the front of the congregation and censes them in the same way.

c. If the arrangement of the church is such that the people are seated facing three sides of the altar, after censing those west of the altar, repeats the action for those on the liturgical north and south. Alternatively, may walk along the edge of the altar platform, censing continually.

d. If preferred, may walk among the people, censing continually.

9. Of Formularies Unique to Rite One

The present Prayer Book has made optional certain formularies in the Rite One eucharist that were required in previous editions of the book:

a. The summary of the law.

b. The comfortable words.

c. The prayer of humble access.

In addition:

a. The Kyries and Gloria may be treated as alternatives.

b. A briefer call to confession is provided.

c. An alternative shorter confession is provided.

d. Alternatives to the prayer for the church may be used.

e. A shorter eucharistic prayer is provided.

Two basic reasons stand behind these changes:

a. To make possible the inclusion of a third lesson and a psalm without making the service longer.

b. To allow for greater variety.

One result of these changes is to make it possible to celebrate the service in the same manner as Rite Two (except that the collect for purity and the blessing are required), and it is suggested that this be done at least on some occasions.

Some of the omissible material might be used on a seasonal basis. Thus:

a. The summary of the law might be used only in Advent and Lent, when the Kyries or Trisagion are required and the Gloria suppressed.

b. The comfortable words might be used only in Advent.

c. The prayer of humble access might be used only in Lent.

It is recommended that frequent use be made of the alternative eucharistic prayer, because it is theologically more adequate, and of form I of the prayers of the people, which, it should be noted, is cast in traditional language.

When presiding from behind the altar, the priest says the prayer of humble access with hands joined and body bowed low.

10. Of Processions

Four movements of persons in the course of the eucharist are sometimes described as processions:

a. The entrance of the clergy and other ministers.

b. The bearing of the gospel book to the ambo.

c. The bringing forward of the offerings of the people.

d. The approach of the people to the altar to receive communion.

What Christian tradition commonly refers to as a procession, however, is a liturgical event in itself. In its classic form it involved the entire congregation, who processed from one church building to another, or from a designated meeting place to the church, or from the church to some other place, such as an outdoor shrine.

The Prayer Book contains two illustrations of this classic form: the Palm Sunday procession, the purpose of which is a public proclamation of the kingship of Christ, and the procession at the consecration of a church, where the congregation walks completely around the building to symbolize the taking possession of it. The Candlemas procession in the *Book of*

Occasional Services is analogous to that appointed for Palm Sunday, and proclaims Christ as the light of the world. The destination in each case is the church, where the eucharist is then celebrated.

To this tradition belongs the deacon's monition to the people, "Let us go forth in peace," and their reply, which indicates their purpose in participating.

In contrast to these processions from one place to another are the directions for "solemn processions" in nineteenth and early twentieth century liturgical manuals, which insisted that processions must begin and end at the altar.

The model for these processions were those that frequently took place before the Sunday mass in the centuries immediately preceding the Reformation, which had as their purpose the offering of prayer at the font, or before the rood, or at a shrine. The reason that they set out from the altar was not, however, a matter of principle, but because that is where the clergy already were, having just completed the office of terce. All present were normally expected to participate (which was easier to do before churches were filled with pews).

A procession before the eucharist on the principal feasts and some other occasions is frequently desired, although in most cases considerations of space make participation by the whole congregation impossible. Unless it is preceded by another service, such as a vigil on Christmas Eve, there is no reason why it should begin at the altar. In most instances, it is best treated as a more elaborate form of the usual entrance, with the choir, if desired, participating, and a longer route being followed.

The monition "Let us go forth in peace" is not recommended before processions in which the congregation does not participate.

It is suitable, and recommended, that a station be made in the course of the procession. At Christmas and Epiphany, the obvious place is a creche. On the other principal feasts, the font is the most appropriate place. At the station a collect is said, preceded, if desired, by a versicle and response.

Banners are suitable in processions, but should be few in number. If the church possesses several, it is usually best to select the one most appropriate to the occasion. Flags are not properly carried in ecclesiastical processions.

If a cope is worn during a procession, it is not retained for the liturgy of the word. At the conclusion of the procession, the priest, having reverenced (and censed) the altar, proceeds to one side of the chancel, exchanges the cope for a chasuble, and then proceeds to the chair. Alternatively, and preferably, the priest wears the chasuble for the procession as well as the eucharist.

When the Great Litany is sung in procession, the cantor who leads it walks immediately behind the crossbearer.

11. Of Practices Not Recommended

In general, the ceremonial suggested in this book is less complex than that which became customary in many parishes over the last hundred years. Part of this is due to a deliberate simplification—in an effort to make the main lines of the liturgy stand out more clearly—and part of it to recovery of more ancient practice, which oftentimes amounts to the same thing.

The following practices are specifically not recommended:

a. The censing of the cross before the censing of the altar at the beginning of the liturgy, and the censing of the priest immediately after it. Instead, the older practice of censing the altar only is recommended.

b. The "offering" or lifting up of the bread and cup by the priest at the offertory — with or without the prayers which accompany this action in the Roman Missal. Our liturgy has recovered the tradition that it is the function of the deacon to prepare the table, and that it is the eucharistic prayer which offers the gifts to God. (See 5.C.4-5,7)

c. Blessing the water to be added to the wine. This practice, which involves a "mystical" understanding of the purpose of the water, came into being after the original meaning—which was a gesture of temperance—had been forgotten.

d. Joining the hands at every occurrence of the name of Jesus in the eucharistic prayer. The practice of bowing the head at the mention of this name does not necessitate the joining of the hands.

e. Extending, raising, and then joining the hands at the words which follow the Sanctus and Benedictus. This gesture dates from a period when the canon or eucharistic prayer was considered to begin at this point, and was a deliberate attempt to indicate a new beginning. Today we have again learned that the prayer begins with the Sursum corda and preface.

f. Elevating the bread and cup after the words of institution. (See 5.C.13)

g. The use of multiple signs of the cross during the eucharistic prayer.

h. Placing a small amount of the consecrated bread in the chalice (the "commixture"). Though retained in the Roman rite, its meaning is not self-evident, and can be explained in several ways. It simply mystifies most worshipers.

i. Making the sign of the cross over the communicants with the consecrated bread before putting it in their hands.

j. Making the sign of the cross at the end of the Gloria in excelsis and of the creed, and at the words "Blessed is he who comes in the name of the Lord." Unlike the sign of the cross at the beginning of the liturgy, and at certain other points, where it helps to explicate what is done and said, these three began as popular devotions. While there can be no objection to individuals crossing themselves when devotion prompts, the invariable use of these three by all present in the chancel suggests that they are required.

There is, however, more to be said about the use of the cross at "Blessed is he." The Sanctus (with Benedictus) is a part of virtually all Christian liturgies, both eastern and western. In no liturgy, save that of Rome from the eleventh century, was a sign of the cross prescribed at this point. The reason for it, Roman scholars have determined, lies somewhere between superstitious fear in the face of Christ's presence under the forms of bread and wine and an outright misinterpretation of the text, the word "blessed" being applied to the worshipers rather than to Christ. The Roman rite has therefore dropped the signing at this point. It is suggested that Episcopalians do the same.

k. The wearing of a biretta during any part of the liturgy, including outdoor processions.

l. "Co-presiding" at the liturgy. This is a recently introduced practice, in which the presidential functions are alternated between two priests in such a manner as to allow each to proclaim an approximately equal amount of the liturgical text. Behind the practice one suspects a lingering medieval notion that a priest cannot be said to participate in the liturgy as a priest without being given words to say.

It should be noted that neither the rubrics of the Prayer Book nor the historic tradition of the church know anything of such a practice, nor do worshipers deserve to have their attention focused on guessing who is to speak next. The proper way for a second priest to participate in the liturgy as a priest is to function as a concelebrating presbyter. (See 2.2)

4

Of Preparations for the Service

1. Of Placing Things in Readiness

The following are placed on the credence:

a. The principal chalice, with its purificator and pall, covered, if desired, with a veil.

b. The corporal, which may be in a burse.

c. The principal paten, unless the bread is to be brought forward on it.

d. Other chalices, with their purificators, and patens, as may be needed.

e. A cruet of water.

f. A cruet or flagon of wine, if there is a possibility that the amount brought forward at the offertory may not be sufficient.

g. Extra bread, if there is a chance it may be needed.

h. The lavabo bowl and towel.

i. Any vessels which may be needed for the reservation of the sacrament.

j. A linen veil or second corporal, if a portion of the sacrament is to remain on the altar after communion.

Near the presidential chair are placed:

a. The sacramentary (altar book), properly marked.

b. A service leaflet, if needed.

c. Hymnals as may be needed.

d. The *Book of Occasional Services* (when needed).

e. The book *Lesser Feasts and Fasts* (on weekdays).

On the lectern-pulpit: The lectionary or a marked Bible, open to the correct page.

In a convenient place:

a. The stand or cushion for the sacramentary (if used).

b. The notebook or binder containing the names and concerns to be read by the deacon or other leader, together with the text of the prayers of the people.

In the church or chancel: Any additional candles to be used.

At the back of the church:

a. The alms basins.

b. The bread and wine to be brought forward.

The following are made ready in the sacristy:

a. Vestments for the ministers.

b. The processional cross and torches (or candles).

c. The gospel book, properly marked.

d. A banner or banners (when used).

e. The thurible and boat (when used).

The candles are lighted.

2. Of a Washing of Hands

The washing of the ministers' hands immediately before vesting is a centuries-old tradition. Part of the reason, no doubt, was spiritual preparation (see, for example, Psalm 24:3-4), and part of it a desire to protect the vestments—a very important consideration in the days before dry cleaning. Today, there is still another reason.

Several times in the course of the twentieth century, questions have been raised about communicable diseases and the use of the common cup. Today, medical experts are agreed that the danger is negligible—even to persons whose immune systems are weakened—especially if the chalice is wiped after each person drinks from it, and then is turned slightly.

A greater potential threat to those whose immune system is suppressed is food, including bread, which has been handled by persons with unwashed hands.

The washing of hands just before vesting should therefore not simply be recommended to ministers of communion, but required.

3. Of Silence While Vesting

In the course of the middle ages, each article of liturgical vesture—from the amice to the chasuble—was given a symbolic meaning, and a series of prayers, expressive of those meanings, were appointed to be said while the vestments were put on.

Today, when we know the real history of the vestments, such prayers seem artificial. They did, however, serve to help the ministers to collect their thoughts in preparation for leading the service.

It is recommended here, for essentially the same reason, that silence be observed in the sacristy, at least from the time that the priest and deacon begin to vest.

Vestments that are not put on straight are a distraction to other worshipers. The acolyte, or a member of the altar guild, properly assists the clergy in this matter. A full-length mirror in the sacristy also helps.

4. Of a Prayer or Office of Preparation

The offering of a prayer before entering the church is common custom. Prayer no. 64 (BCP p. 833) is frequently used for the purpose. On days when it will not be used in the public service, the collect for purity is an excellent choice.

Sometimes other devotions are used as well, concluding with a collect. In some places Hymn 504 (or 502), Veni Creator Spiritus—which in the Sarum Missal was associated with the collect for purity—is recited. In others the following brief office is said:

a. The invocation "In the Name of the Father . . . ."

b. The antiphon "I will go to the altar of God, to the God of my joy and gladness."

c. Psalm 43 (or 42:1-2 and 43:3-6) with Gloria Patri.

d. A repetition of the antiphon.

e. A collect.

All such devotions pertain only to the priest and others who will be entering the church in procession. They should be said behind closed doors in order that they may not be overheard by those assembled in the church.

5

The Service in Detail

The Holy Eucharist consists of two major but inter-related parts: the liturgy of the word, which derives from the practice of the synagogue, and the liturgy of the table, the structure of which derives from that of Jewish formal meals.

Part A.

Of the Entrance Rite

In the early centuries, the liturgy began with the first reading, preceded only by a brief salutation, such as "The Lord be with you," or "Peace be with you."

With the transfer of Christian worship from a setting in private homes or "house churches" (houses converted into places of worship) to public buildings, a desire for a more formal beginning began to be felt. In the course of the fifth century, accordingly, various preliminaries were gradually added. In the western use which is the ancestor of our Prayer Book rite, the oldest of these is the entrance chant. Subsequently, the collect before the readings, the Kyrie eleison, and the Gloria in excelsis were added. All these elements appear in the present Prayer Book service.

It is desirable that all present stand throughout the entrance rite. On occasions when the penitential order is used, the people may kneel for the confession and absolution, but should then stand for the Gloria in excelsis, Kyrie eleison, or Trisagion, and the collect.

1. Of the Entrance Hymn

In the Episcopal Church, the liturgy usually begins with a congregational hymn, rather than with a psalm or anthem. During it, the ministers enter in procession and go to their places. The purpose of the hymn, however, is not merely to cover this action, but to begin the celebration and to foster a sense of unity among the assembled worshipers. To accomplish such a purpose, it is essential that the hymn be either familiar or rehearsed beforehand.

On most Sundays in the year (the "green" Sundays), there is no necessity for this hymn to be selected with reference to the appointed readings, which, after all, have not yet been heard. Subtle references to them—though satisfying to the person selecting the hymn—usually escape the attention of the worshipers. The best choice is frequently a hymn about the Lord's Day (*The Hymnal 1982*, nos. 47-52) or a general hymn of praise or invocation.

On other Sundays, and on holy days, the hymn also serves to focus attention on the season or feast being celebrated, and the best choice is usually a hymn associated exclusively with the season or occasion. This has long been common practice in Advent, and it is desirable that it also become the practice in Easter season. There is little hope that the Prayer Book's stress on Easter as a season, rather than as just a day or an octave, will be realized until congregations come to expect to sing Easter hymns at the beginning of Sunday services right up to the Day of Pentecost. (On the seventh Sunday, a hymn suitable for the Ascension might be used instead.)

The number of hymns proper to Lent is small, and it is suitable to use one of them at the entrance on only two or three of the Sundays. Carefully chosen hymns from elsewhere in the hymnal will serve for the other Sundays. On some of the Sundays, such as the first (or second) and fifth, the Great Litany may appropriately be used in place of a hymn. The custom of using a "Jerusalem hymn" (such as no. 624 or 623) on the fourth Sunday is a commendable one.

On most occasions, the choir should be in place before the hymn begins, in order to perform the important function of giving vigorous leadership to the congregational singing.

2. Of an Entrance Psalm or Anthem

As alternatives to an entrance hymn, the Prayer Book provides for the use of a psalm or anthem.

The use of a whole psalm at the entrance of the ministers was an innovation of the 1549 Prayer Book. The practice lasted only three and a half years, however, since it was suppressed by the Prayer Book of 1552. No reason for this was stated at the time, but it must be admitted that the selection of psalms made in 1549 was less than satisfactory, involving, as it did, the use of successive sections of Psalm 119 on the first twenty-two Sundays after Trinity Sunday.

Under the present rubric, any suitable psalm, or portion of a psalm, may be used. If desired, the selection may conclude with Gloria Patri (BCP p. 406).

The ancient repertory of entrance chants (introits) is also covered by the present rubric. In that tradition, no attempt was made to use a complete psalm. The introit began with an antiphon, sung by the choir, which the choir then repeated after each verse of the appointed psalm. The verses themselves were sung by a cantor, and only as many verses as were needed were used. When the ministers had arrived at their places in the chancel, the cantor, instead of singing the next verse, sang the Gloria Patri, after which the choir repeated the antiphon for the last time. (Under the Prayer Book rubric, p. 406, the addition of the Gloria Patri is optional.)

Some parishes may wish to make occasional use of an entrance psalm. One appropriate time would be the first five Sundays in Lent (with the exception of those on which the Great Litany is to be used).

The other alternative is an anthem sung by the choir, which is the historic custom of the Ambrosian liturgy of northern Italy. It is desirable that the anthem selected be long enough to cover the entrance procession (and censing of the altar) but not significantly longer.

All of the options described in this section assume that the choir is in place before the singing begins. Originally, when the entrance chant was sung by the choir, the next musical piece in the liturgy (Kyrie eleison, Trisagion, or Gloria in excelsis) involved singing by the congregation.

3. Of the Entrance of the Ministers

During the singing of the hymn, psalm, or anthem, the ministers enter, preferably through the midst of the people, in the following order:

a. The thurifer with smoking censer (if incense is used).

b. Two candlebearers with lighted candles or torches. Between them, the acolyte bearing the processional cross.

(c. The choir, if not already in place.)

d. Additional servers, if needed.

e. The reader(s) and cantor, if vested.

f. The lay eucharistic ministers.

g. The deacon bearing the gospel book.

h. The concelebrating presbyters, if any are present.

i. The priest-celebrant.

If incense is used at the entrance, the priest puts some into the censer before the procession begins.

If the way is narrow, the candlebearers precede the cross. If there are not enough servers, either the cross or the candles may be omitted. When possible, however, preference should be given to the candles because of their traditional use in the gospel procession.

The deacon, if not bearing the gospel book, walks beside the priest (normally to the right).

In the absence of a deacon, the gospel book may be carried by a concelebrating presbyter or a vested reader. Alternatively, it may be placed on the altar before the service begins. The book is carried, and placed on the altar, with the opening to the left.

It is preferable that the priest, as president of the assembly, walk with hands joined (i.e., without a hymnal), so as not to appear uninterested in those who are present. The same is true of a deacon not bearing the gospel book.

On arrival before the altar:

a. The candlebearers and crossbearer pause very briefly and, without reverencing the altar, put the cross and candles in their proper places.

b. Others bow low (or may genuflect if the sacrament is reserved in the chancel) before going to their places.

c. The deacon reverences the altar simultaneously with the priest. If bearing the gospel book, however, the deacon omits the reverence, and immediately places the book on the altar.

The ceremonies of placing the gospel book on the altar and kissing the altar, when observed, may be done either at the front of the altar (the people's side) or while standing behind it. In the latter case, the deacon leads the way (to the right) and the priest, after reverencing the altar, follows. Then, standing together behind it, the deacon places the book on it (closed and lying flat). They may both then kiss the altar.

If the altar is to be censed, the priest, standing at the center of it (whether in front of it or behind it), turns to face the thurifer, who presents the censer. Taking the censer, the priest walks around the altar counterclockwise, censing continually, and then returns the censer to the thurifer. The deacon, meanwhile, stands aside, facing the altar.

The priest then goes to the chair, and the deacon to the seat at the priest's right.

For liturgical gestures appropriate to the sections that follow, see chapter 6, the Synopsis of Ceremonies.

4. Of the Opening Acclamation

The Prayer Book provides three opening acclamations, only one of which is to be used on a given occasion. The one for Lent is also for use on "other penitential occasions," by which is not meant the season of Advent (which is not accounted a time of penitence), but special services at which penitence is to be stressed, such as services in the interest of social justice or reconciliation.

5. Of the Collect for Purity

In Rite Two this collect is optional, which makes possible the recovery of the tradition that the collect of the day is the opening prayer of the liturgy. Its treasured place in Anglican piety, however, would suggest that it be used on at least some occasions in the year. One such use is suggested below (see section 7).

6. Of the Penitential Order

The Prayer Book provides a penitential order for use at the beginning of the liturgy which, in effect, places the confession and absolution at the point in the service which the collect for purity would otherwise occupy (p. 351). The rubrics, however, do not make any suggestions about its use. The reason for this provision is a long-standing disagreement (of several centuries' duration) about the most suitable place for a confession of sin. Most Anglicans appear to prefer a point in the service following the readings and sermon, the confession being understood as one of the people's responses to the proclamation of the word of God. Others believe that it should ordinarily come at the beginning of the service as a preparation for receiving the word as well as the sacrament. Since congregational confessions of sin did not enter the liturgy until the time of the Reformation, there is no ancient tradition to appeal to in the matter.

Some priests make no use at all of the provision to say the confession at the earlier point, and this is a wholly proper usage. Others use it during Lent in the belief that it calls greater attention to the penitential nature of the season. Still others argue that the Lenten opening acclamation, followed by the collect for purity and the Kyries or Trisagion is, in itself, a convincing penitential beginning; and that the confession should be said later in the service. They also believe that the force of the absolution seems weakened when it is followed by the Kyries or Trisagion, with their cries for mercy.

Another way of making occasional use of the penitential order is to use it on some of the "green" Sundays of the year, such as those after Epiphany, when the absolution can be followed immediately by the Gloria in excelsis.

7. Of a Sprinkling with Baptismal Water in Easter Season

The Roman rite provides for a sprinkling of the congregation—a reminder of baptism—on all Sundays in the year, in place of the confession of sin (which always comes at this early point in that liturgy). The ceremony as a whole is not likely to be adopted by Episcopalians for two reasons: (a) it is long, being preceded and followed by (rather didactic) prayers, and (b) the Prayer Book expects that, except "on occasion," the confession of sin will be a regular part of the service.

The recovery of the association of baptism with Easter, however, makes attractive the use of such a sprinkling during Easter season—though without the Roman prayers. It is also a season in which the confession of sin is appropriately omitted.

When desired, the ceremony may take the following form. Immediately after the collect for purity—which fittingly introduces the sprinkling—the priest, holding the vat of water in one hand, takes the sprinkler from it with the other, touches the forehead with it, sprinkles the others present in the chancel, then walks among the people (down the aisle), sprinkling alternately to the right and to the left, and dipping the sprinkler into the water at frequent intervals. In the meantime, the anthem "I saw water" may be sung (see 15.2). At the conclusion of the sprinkling, the Gloria in excelsis is begun.

If, on Easter Day and the Day of Pentecost, the renewal of baptismal vows is used in place of the Nicene Creed, the sprinkling is appropriately postponed until immediately after it.

If Holy Baptism is administered, the sprinkling is postponed until after the baptism.

Should there be no baptismal water available, the priest—before the congregation arrives—may set apart water for the sprinkling (see 15.4).

8. Of the Gloria in excelsis

Gloria in excelsis is one of the oldest of Christian hymns, and may date from as early as the second century. The custom of singing it at festal celebrations of the eucharist began in the fifth century. Its appropriateness to Christmas season is secured by its opening line (Luke 2:14), and its acclamation of Christ as the victorious Lamb, who takes away the sin of the world and sits at the right hand of the Father, doubtless explains its traditional association with Sundays and Easter Season.

Using the rubric on page 406 of the Prayer Book as a starting point, the use of the Gloria is here recommended on:

a. All Sundays, except those in Advent and Lent.

b. All principal and major feasts.

c. Occasions of local festivity, such as patronal and dedication feasts and weddings (where it may be the "hymn" provided for on page 425).

d. All weekdays between Christmas Day and the first Sunday after the Epiphany, and between Easter Day and the Day of Pentecost.

The Prayer Book permits the use of another song of praise in place of the Gloria in excelsis (p. 356). As the rubric in the Easter Vigil indicates (p. 294), what is intended is some other "prose hymn" or canticle, rather than a metrical hymn. In using this permission, care must be taken in selecting the text, since some of the Prayer Book canticles are not, in fact, songs of praise.

It may be questioned, however, whether this is a point in the service where much variety is wanted. In one sense, the Gloria in excelsis functions in the same way as does the Venite at Morning Prayer: it presents the worshipers with a text known to all, and which they can readily make their own. It is also a much loved text that people do not seem to tire of repeating. Varying the song of praise is therefore not recommended here. Should a single alternative be desired, Canticle 18, which is also a song addressed to God and to the Lamb, might be used on some of the Sundays after Pentecost.

Originally, the Gloria was sung by the entire congregation. Many choir settings also exist, and there is no reason not to use them on occasion. The Prayer Book specifically permits the use of "previously authorized texts" for the corresponding ones in Rite Two when music composed for them is being used (p. 14). The Gloria may therefore, when desired, be sung either in the traditional English version given in Rite One or in Latin.

9. Of Kyrie eleison and the Trisagion

The Prayer Book requires the use of one of these two chants whenever the Gloria in excelsis (or other song of praise) is not sung or said.

If the Gloria is used as suggested above in section 8, Kyrie eleison or the Trisagion will take its place on:

a. The Sundays of Advent and Lent.

b. All weekdays, except those occurring between Christmas Day and 1 Epiphany and in Easter season.

c. All lesser feasts, except those that fall in Easter season.

Kyrie eleison is first found in Christian liturgy in the east, where it is used as a congregational response (addressed to Christ) to a series of biddings addressed to the people, in exactly the same way as in our first form of the prayers of the people (BCP p. 383). In a variant eastern form, it is repeated several times in succession at the conclusion of a litany addressed directly to Christ.

For a time, a litany of this second type was used in the Roman liturgy immediately after the entrance chant (the prayers of the people in their traditional place before the offertory being dropped). Later, the litany itself was dropped, leaving only the Kyries that concluded it. These, together with invocations of Christe eleison, were sung by the clergy and repeated by the people for as long as the bishop or priest presiding thought appropriate to the occasion. Still later, the people's repetitions were dropped, the number of repetitions fixed at nine (Christe eleison being used for the middle three), and the piece assigned to the choir. This ninefold performance remained the standard up to and including the Prayer Book of 1549. From 1552 until the twentieth century, the ten commandments with their responses were used instead.

The 1928 Prayer Book reintroduced the text in threefold form, and the present Prayer Book, in addition to permitting its use in the original Greek, provides for sixfold and ninefold performance as well. From a devotional point of view, threefold settings are seldom satisfactory. They are usually not long enough to engage the worshipers' attention in a serious way. Sixfold or ninefold settings are therefore recommended.

The Trisagion is a text drawn from the entrance rite of the Byzantine liturgy. It became widely popular, and was taken into regular use by many other liturgies, both eastern and western. The chief exception is the Roman rite, in which it is used only on Good Friday. The present Prayer Book is the first Anglican liturgy to include it. The rubrics (p. 406) provide that it may be sung three times, which is recommended here, or antiphonally, which is the traditional western method (no example of which, unfortunately, is given in the present hymnal). In this method, the text is divided into three parts, each of which is sung twice, either alternately by two groups of singers or between a cantor and the people, as follows:

> Holy God,
> *Holy God,*
> Holy and Mighty,
> *Holy and Mighty,*
> Holy Immortal One, have mercy upon us.
> *Holy Immortal One, have mercy upon us.*

10. Of the Collect of the Day

The collect of the day concludes the entrance rite and introduces the liturgy of the word.

From the Last Sunday after Pentecost through Trinity Sunday, the Sunday collects are usually related in a thematic way to the gospel of the day. On the other Sundays after Pentecost they are general prayers, which may or may not relate to the appointed lessons and psalm.

Only one collect is used at a given service. (The only exceptions are ordinations and funerals.)

The observance of a brief period of silent prayer between "Let us pray" and the collect is strongly recommended.

Part B

Of the Liturgy of the Word

The public reading of the Scriptures is a part of our inheritance from Judaism, and the adoption of the practice by the early church is attested to in the New Testament (1 Tim. 4:13). In the earliest period, the readings were, necessarily, from the Old Testament only. Later, as distinctively Christian writings appeared, they were read also. St. Paul's letters to the churches were intended to be read aloud to the faithful (Col. 4:16, 1 Thess. 5:27), and the gospels were compiled for this express purpose.

Originally, the number of readings was not fixed, and practice varied considerably. With the passage of time, three readings became a widely accepted norm, the first being from the Old Testament (with some exceptions), the second from the New Testament (other than the gospels), and the third from the gospel. On the great feasts, and on special occasions, the readings were chosen for their appropriateness to the occasion. At other times, books were read "in course," a given epistle, for example, being read in installments at successive services.

Unfortunately, in the course of the middle ages, the number of readings was reduced to two in most places, with the result that the Old Testament was rarely heard at Sunday services. Only in the twentieth century was the tradition of three readings widely recovered.

Recent times have also seen the recovery (in western churches) of the practice of singing a psalm between the readings, a custom frequently mentioned in the writings of the church fathers.

1. Of the Prayer Book Lectionary

The present Prayer Book lectionary is a revised version of the Roman *Ordo Lectionum Missae*, prepared, in consultation with scholars of other denominations, including our own, after the Second Vatican Council. Versions of it are also in use in the Lutheran, Presbyterian, Methodist, and other North American churches.

The lectionary is arranged in a three-year cycle, year A being the year of Matthew, year B the year of Mark, and year C the year of Luke. On the Sundays after Epiphany and after Pentecost in each year, the appointed gospel is read "semi-continuously," that is, "in course," but omitting some of the passages that will be read at other times, or which also appear in one of the other gospels. (Because the gospel of Mark is too short, a series of readings from John is interpolated after Proper 12.) The epistles are also read "semi-continuously" during these two seasons, and there is therefore no thematic connection between them and the gospels. The Old Testament readings are chosen to match the gospel or, occasionally, the epistle.

In the seasons of Advent, Christmas, Lent, and Easter, and on holy days, the readings are selected with reference to the season or occasion. In addition to readings from the gospel of the year, much use is made of John's gospel. Easter season and Lent also have some special features, most of which are based on ancient traditions.

In Easter season, the Acts of the Apostles is read in place of the Old Testament in all three years. (The Old Testament passages listed as alternatives are intended for use at Morning Prayer.) The second readings are from 1 Peter, 1 John, and Revelation. The gospel readings are accounts of the resurrection or selections from John's gospel.

In Lent, the Old Testament readings are a series in themselves. In each year, they present a synopsis of the Old Testament history of salvation which, traditionally, is part of the instruction given to candidates for baptism. In year A, the stories of Nicodemus, the Samaritan woman, the man born blind, and Lazarus are read. These accounts from John's gospel are particularly important in the church's understanding of the meaning of Holy Baptism, and look forward to the Easter Vigil.

On weekdays, the normal expectation is that only one lesson will be read before the gospel. See, for example, the Prayer Book provisions for Monday through Saturday of Easter Week (p. 894), and the proper for the weekdays of Lent and Easter, and for the lesser feasts, in the book *Lesser Feasts and Fasts.*

2. Of the Place of Reading

Originally, all the Scripture readings, including the gospel, were read from the same place, a lectern or pulpit known as an "ambo." Because this practice emphasizes the unity of the word of God, it is given pride of place in the rubrics of the Prayer Book by being listed first (p. 406), and it is the practice recommended here.

The Prayer Book also permits the reading of the gospel "from the midst of the congregation," a practice which, in the form familiar to Episcopalians, first became popular in the 1950s. At that time, it was presented as a helpful alternative to the prevailing practice of reading the gospel from the altar, which was usually located at some distance from the people. No thought, apparently, was given to the possibility of reading it from the lectern, perhaps because lecterns were then associated only with morning and evening prayer. At any rate, it must be pointed out that reading in the midst of the congregation has distinct disadvantages. Frequently, it makes it difficult to hear. Just as importantly, it makes it difficult for many people—and most children—to see the person reading it.

The original "gospel procession" was a procession from the altar, where the gospel book had rested since the beginning of the service, to the ambo. This is the practice recommended here. Should the route be short, because the ambo or lectern is located at a corner of the altar platform, there is nothing to prevent the procession descending to the floor of the church, turning and walking in front of the ambo, and then approaching it from the side furthest from the altar.

3. Of the Readings before the Gospel and the Psalm

The present Prayer Book has recovered the tradition of assigning the lessons that precede the gospel to lay persons. See the section on the ministry of lectors (2.5). Only when there are no competent lay persons present to fulfill this ministry should priests or deacons do so.

There is no need for the lector to approach the lectern-pulpit during the collect of the day. Following the collect, the congregation sits, and it is fitting that they be given a moment to make themselves comfortable. While they do so, the lector can approach the ambo in an unhurried and dignified fashion.

In most places the lessons are read, rather than chanted. It is suitable, however, for the lector to sing the concluding acclamation, "The Word of the Lord," in order that the people may sing the reply. It should be noted that the acclamation, "The Word of the Lord," refers to the passage that has been read, rather than to the book from which it is read. The practice of lifting up the lectionary or Bible while these words are sung or said is therefore not recommended. A period of silence of at least one full minute's duration is suggested after the acclamation "The Word of the Lord" and the people's response.

The psalm (sometimes called the "gradual") that follows the first reading is intended as an integral part of the liturgy of the word—commenting on or responding to the appointed lections. Traditionally, it is sung by a cantor from the lectern-pulpit. The congregation remains seated and sings the appointed refrain after the cantor has sung it and after each verse or group of verses.

Other methods of singing the psalm are also appropriate and, if desired, different methods may be used at different times. On some occasions the psalm might be sung by the choir or a cantor to an elaborate chant without refrain. At other times it might be sung to a simple chant by all present. An anthem setting of the whole piece or of the most germane verses might also be used on occasion.

As the rubrics point out, it is the shorter version of the psalm, or the alternative psalm (or canticle) that is recommended for the eucharist (BCP p. 888).

When the psalm is read rather than sung, the rubrics suggest—because the selections are short—that they be read in unison by all present (BCP p. 582). It is recommended here that the reader of the first lesson announce and begin the psalm, in order that the attention of the congregation not be diverted from the lectern to the place where the priest is sitting.

Traditionally, and desirably, Gloria Patri is not used with this psalm. (The reference to Gloria Patri on page 406 of the Prayer Book is not to this psalm, but to a psalm sung at the entrance of the ministers. Note that the rubric in question precedes those that pertain to the Kyrie eleison and the Gloria in excelsis.)

On weekdays, when only one reading precedes the gospel, it is important that the function of the psalm not be undermined by making preparations for the gospel during it. All, except the cantor or person who began it, should remain seated until the psalm is finished. If there is to be a formal gospel procession, an alleluia or tract may be sung (see 5 below), or the procession may take place in silence.

4. Of the Sequence Hymn

The singing of a metrical hymn during the liturgy of the word is a practice that first appeared in the tenth century. Prior to that time, only an alleluia or tract (see 5 below) was sung at this point in the service.

Unfortunately, the tenth-century liturgists who began the practice placed the hymn after the alleluia, thus obscuring the latter's traditional association with the gospel. It is suggested here that the sequence, when used, precede the alleluia or tract, in order that the latter may serve its original function of accompanying the gospel procession. Preparations for the procession, such as putting incense into the thurible and bringing in torches, appropriately take place toward the conclusion of the hymn.

In places where an alleluia or tract is not used, the gospel procession takes place during the sequence hymn.

Of all the hymns sung in the course of the liturgy, the sequence is the one that obviously needs to be related to the proper of the day. Indeed, many of the new hymns in *The Hymnal 1982* were included for the purpose of ensuring that there would be at least one such hymn available for each proper. The sequence may be chosen to reflect one or more of the themes of the lesson which has immediately preceded or, equally suitably, may anticipate the gospel which is to follow. (Hymns that relate only to the first reading are more appropriately used at the entrance, or later in the service.)

5. Of the Alleluia or Tract

The singing of alleluia in anticipation of the gospel can be traced back to the third century and may be even older.

One traditional form involves the use of a psalm or portion of a psalm, sung by a cantor, to which the congregation responds with "alleluia" (or "hallelujah") one or more times after the cantor has sung it and again after each verse.

The other (and more usual) form consists of only one verse, which may or may not be taken from a psalm. The people repeat the alleluia after the cantor has sung it and again after the verse.

In Lent, when alleluia is not used at the liturgy, a tract is sung instead. This consists of selected verses of a psalm (or else a short psalm) sung by a cantor or by the choir, without refrain. (Another alternative is a single verse of Scripture, sung by the cantor or choir.)

All stand for the alleluia or tract. If a sequence hymn has not preceded, and the route of the gospel procession is long, it is desirable that incense (if used) be put on before the singing begins so that the chant will not end before the procession arrives at the ambo.

6. Of the Gospel

In the tradition of the church, the reading of the gospel is attended by marks of special honor. All stand for the reading, which is preceded and followed by acclamations directed to Christ, who is thereby acknowledged to be present in the reading of his gospel. All face the gospel book, and the person reading from it, throughout the reading and during the two acclamations.

The two lights carried at the gospel are both a token of joy and a symbol of Christ, the light of the world (John 8:12). The use of incense is also appropriate. The use of a processional cross at this point is not desirable. The original purpose of the lights was to accompany the gospel book, a purpose that is obscured when a cross is carried, since they appear to be accompanying it instead. A cross, moreover, tends to call attention away from the book.

It is the prerogative of a deacon to read the gospel (BCP p. 354). In the absence of a deacon it is read by a concelebrating presbyter, if one is present, or by the priest.

The ancient practice of blessing the deacon who is to read the gospel is specifically recommended. Two alternative formulas are provided for this purpose in the Synopsis of Ceremonies (6.18). A priest who is to read the gospel does not receive a blessing (except when the bishop is present) but, instead, may say the silent prayer suggested.

After receiving the blessing, and not before, the deacon takes the gospel book from the altar, from the front or back as may be more convenient, and, preceded by the (thurifer and) candlebearers, carries it, closed and held high, to the lectern-pulpit. On arrival, the deacon places the book on the stand and opens it. The candlebearers stand on either side, or on the floor below, facing the deacon. The thurifer stands nearby.

Customarily, all present make a sign of the cross with the right thumb on the forehead, lips, and breast when the gospel is announced.

After announcing the gospel, the deacon may cense the book.

In most churches, the gospel is read rather than chanted. It is suitable, however, to sing the announcement formula at the beginning, and the words, "The Gospel of the Lord," at the end, in order that the people may sing the acclamations that follow. The practice of elevating the book at "The Gospel of the Lord" is not recommended.

Where it is the custom to kiss the book, the reader lifts it to a comfortable height and kisses the text; then replaces the book on the desk and closes it. Depending on local preference, the book is then returned to the altar, taken to the credence, placed on a shelf within the pulpit, or left on the lectern.

7. Of the Sermon

The present Prayer Book deliberately makes no provision for a hymn (or anything else) to intrude between the gospel and the sermon. This exclusion raises serious questions about the practice, sometimes seen, of singing the opening stanzas of a hymn during the gospel procession, and the remaining stanzas after the gospel—while the procession returns and the preacher goes to the pulpit. Such a practice also does little justice to the integrity—and frequently to the sense—of the text of the hymn.

If something is truly needed to "cover" the return of the gospel procession, instrumental music is suggested. It is important, however, that what is played not be a recapitulation of the music of the sequence hymn, which would draw the attention of the congregation away from the gospel, or any other music that brings words to mind.

An invocation or prayer before the sermon is not a necessity. This practice appears to derive from a period when sermons were frequently preached apart from the liturgy, and when sermons within the liturgy were regarded as an addition rather than as an integral part of it. There is nothing in the rubrics to prevent the preacher from simply asking the congregation to be seated.

Similarly, there is no need for a concluding invocation or ascription. A number of the sermons of the church fathers conclude in a manner similar to the ending of a collect ("through Jesus Christ our Lord" or "who lives and reigns for ever and ever"), a practice that frequently inspired the composition of highly effective concluding paragraphs and provoked a congregational Amen.

In the early church, following Jewish custom, the preacher usually sat in a chair to preach (see Luke 4:20-21). Even today, it is sometimes effective to preach from a chair placed at the entrance to the chancel. At weekday services, when the sermon is to be brief, the preacher might stand at the chancel steps. At principal services in most churches, however, the pulpit is the only place from which the preacher can be both heard and seen by all present. It also makes it possible for those whose hearing is impaired to read the preacher's lips.

At most services, it is desirable that the priest presiding at the service also be the preacher, thus underscoring the intimate connection and parallel between the "breaking" of the word of God in the sermon and the breaking of bread for communion.

If desired, a brief period of silent reflection may follow the sermon, all being seated.

8. Of the Nicene Creed

The use of the Nicene Creed at the liturgy was a gradual development, being adopted in various parts of the church in the period from the fifth to the eleventh centuries. Earlier tradition had regarded the eucharistic prayer as the church's profession of faith.

The rubrics require the use of the creed on Sundays (except Palm Sunday) and other major feasts (p. 358). It is not used on other days.

A bow of the head is traditional at the mention of "Jesus." A low bow at the words "By the power of the Holy Spirit . . . and was made man" is also recommended.

When the priest-celebrant is the preacher, it may be found convenient to lead the creed from the pulpit or from the place where the announcements are to be made, the priest facing the altar.

At all eucharists on the four days of the year recommended for the administration of Holy Baptism—if there are none to be baptized—the renewal of baptismal vows appropriately takes the place of the Nicene Creed (rubric, BCP p. 312). The priest leads the renewal either from the font or from the chancel step, and afterwards may sprinkle the people with water.

If the creed is sung, a simple congregational setting should be used.

9. Of Announcements

The rubrics provide for the making of necessary announcements at four possible points in the liturgy: (1) before the service, (2) after the creed, (3) before the offertory, (4) at the end of the service (BCP p. 407).

There are times when it is necessary to make one or more announcements before the service begins. The classic case is occasions when baptism is to be administered but a service leaflet giving page numbers has not been distributed. If the people have not been told that the service begins on page 299 rather than page 355, they will not be ready to join in the versicles that follow the opening acclamation.

There are also times when an announcement at the end of the service (preferably just before the blessing and dismissal) is appropriate. If, for example, a parish meeting is to take place following the coffee hour, the fact is best mentioned at this point—more people are likely to remember it.

While local or pastoral considerations may sometimes make it necessary to make announcements before the offertory, it is suggested that the usual place be after the creed, and for the following reasons:

a. The exchange of the peace is as much the beginning of the eucharistic liturgy as it is the conclusion of the liturgy of the word. To follow it by announcements is to interrupt what should be perceived as a "hinge" between the two major parts of the rite.

b. Making the announcements after the creed makes it possible to use what has been announced as subjects for intercession. (Indeed, some have questioned whether anything should be announced in church that does not deserve to be prayed about.) When a beloved parishioner has suddenly died, for example, it is more appropriate to announce the fact before the prayers of the people are offered than to stun people with the information by including the name in a list of the dead who are to be commemorated. Notices of coming weddings and announcements of the birth of children are other examples of what is appropriately made known at this point.

10. Of a Sentence of Invitation before the Prayers

The rubrics specify that the priest may introduce the prayers of the people with a sentence of invitation related to the occasion, or the season, or the proper of the day (BCP p. 383). While not required, the occasional use of this provision can help the congregation focus on its priestly task of recalling before God the needs of both church and world.

The use of the provision is especially helpful at weekday services at which (because of the constraints of time) there is no sermon. In these circumstances, the invitation can well be extended to three or four sentences, and can relate a phrase or theme of one of the lessons to a call to prayer.

The most effective invitations are usually those that have been carefully crafted, and either memorized or read from a card or notebook.

11. Of the Reading of Names and Concerns

The reading aloud of the names of persons to be prayed for, and for whose "intentions" the eucharist is to be offered (along with the intentions of all present) is an ancient feature of Christian liturgy that has been revived in a number of parishes. While some of the forms of the prayers of the people provide for the insertion of names or concerns by members of the congregation, not all of them do. It is, moreover, frequently awkward for the person leading the prayers to add lists of names and concerns at the appropriate points. It is therefore suggested that such lists be read before the prayers begin, a practice which also has the advantage of informing the congregation about particular needs before they join in the prayers.

The following, or some similar procedure, is recommended:

a. All stand, and the deacon or other leader says "Our prayers are asked for those preparing to be baptized (confirmed) (received)" and then reads the names of those for whom prayer is asked. Then, as needed and appropriate (each bidding being followed by a list of names) "Let us pray for the sick," "Let us pray for those in special need," "Let us thank God for...," "Let us remember those who have died," "Let us remember those whose memorial of death falls this week."

b. Then, unless the form of intercession to be used includes places where the congregation can insert names and concerns, the deacon or leader says "Let us offer other names and concerns, either silently or aloud." Sufficient time is then allowed for the people to do so.

c. The deacon or person appointed then begins the prayers.

Anciently, it was usually the deacon who read the names and led the prayers. The Prayer Book rubrics provide that the prayers may be led either by a deacon or a lay person (p. 354). Whenever a deacon is present, however, it is desirable that he or she (because of the special responsibility of the diaconate for ministry to the poor, the needy, and the sick) take an active role at this point in the service.

If desired, an appointed lay person might share this ministry with the deacon. On some occasions the list of names might be read by the lay person and the prayers themselves led by the deacon. On other occasions the opposite procedure might be used.

12. Of the Prayers of the People

The Prayer Book provides six forms for the prayers of the people. These may be used as printed, or may be adapted to the occasion. When insertions are made, care should be taken that they are appropriately placed. In form I, for example, a petition for the newly baptized should be inserted among the prayers for the church, i.e., either before or after the petition for the bishop, clergy, and people (top of p. 384).

The forms are also intended to serve as models. Thus, a form prepared for a particular occasion, or which contains petitions especially suitable to the season of the church year being celebrated, is also fully legitimate. All that is required is that the form include the topics listed on pages 359 and 383.

Of the forms provided, forms I and V are the most inclusive in their range of intercessions, and are therefore the ones most appropriate for Sunday celebrations. These two forms also provide for the naming of saints in the concluding bidding. In addition to the Virgin Mary and the patron of the parish—who are appropriately commemorated whenever desired—a saint mentioned in the readings (John the Baptist on 2 and 3 Advent, Joseph at Christmas and on some other days, Thomas on 2 Easter) may also be named at this point. Except in Holy Week and Easter Week (see BCP p. 17), mention may also be made of a "lesser" saint whose calendar date falls on the Sunday being celebrated, or of a "major" saint whose liturgical observance is to be transferred to a later date under the rules of precedence (for example, Andrew, when 1 Advent falls on November 30).

When the Great Litany is used at the beginning of the liturgy, it is permissible to omit the prayers of the people completely (p. 406). It is suggested, however, that they be offered in the following brief form, in order to take individual needs into account.

After the reading of names and concerns, the deacon says to the people: "Let us remember before God those who have been commended to our prayers, and let us commend ourselves, and one another, and all our life to Christ our God." After the people have made the usual reply, a period of silence, longer than usual, is observed, after which the priest says a concluding collect.

It is desirable that—in accordance with ancient tradition—all stand for the prayers on Sundays and in Easter season. Kneeling is appropriate on weekdays, and especially on the weekdays of Lent.

13. Of the Collect after the Prayers

The concluding collect is said by the priest presiding at the liturgy (BCP p. 394). Eight general collects are provided, but any suitable one may be used. On the Sundays in Lent and in Easter Season, one of the seasonal collects given in *Lesser Feasts and Fasts* may appropriately be used here. It is preferable that they be concluded with a short ending, such as "through Christ our Lord. *Amen,*" or "who lives and reigns for ever and ever. *Amen.*"

On the weekdays of Lent, the collect of a lesser feast may be used to conclude the prayers of the people (LFF, p. 20). The practice is not recommended for Sundays (though the saint's name may be mentioned—see section 13 above).

14. Of the Confession of Sin

The Prayer Book requires that those who come to communion shall have examined their lives, repented of their sins, and be in love and charity with all people. To those whose consciences are burdened, it counsels confession before a priest. For the correction of the impenitent, it provides for the refusal of communion until such time as proof of repentance has been shown (BCP pp. 860, 317, 409). All of these provisions are part of the normative tradition of the Church, and are clearly rooted in the teaching of the New Testament (1 Cor. 11:27-29, Matt. 18:15-17, James 5:16, John 20:22-23).

It frequently comes as a surprise to Episcopalians to discover that ancient liturgies contained nothing like a general confession of sin. Repentance, when needed, was something done before one came to the eucharist. The sign of reconciliation with God and one's brothers and sisters was not a general absolution, but the exchange of the peace.

The exhortation on page 316 of the Prayer Book contains valuable teaching that people need to know. It is suggested for use at this point in the service on the second Sunday in Lent (a day on which the collect is particularly appropriate to the practice). The concluding phrase of the exhortation takes the place of the bidding, "Let us confess our sins. . . ."

The rubrics provide for the omission of the confession "on occasion (BCP p. 359). As noted above in 5.A.7, it is appropriately omitted during the fifty days of Easter, and it may also be omitted at other times of special festivity. It can also be omitted when a confession has been said at a preceding daily office or at a special service of preparation for communion.

The trial use liturgies of the 1970s specified that when the confession of sin was omitted, a penitential petition was to be included in the prayers of the people. The Prayer Book contains no such requirement, but the practice may be followed where desired.

15. Of the Peace

The exchange of the peace between Christians is a practice that dates back to the time of the New Testament (Rom. 16:16; 1 Cor. 16:20; 2 Cor. 13:12; 1 Thess. 5:26; 1 Peter 5:14). It is a sign of love, affection, and greeting, but supremely it is a sharing of that peace bestowed by the risen Christ (John 20:19, 21, 26).

It is also a sign of reconciliation and, in the early church, an unwillingness to exchange it with any of the faithful assembled was considered to disqualify one from participation in the eucharistic sacrifice and from receiving communion (Matt. 5:23-24).

One of the advantages of omitting the confession of sin on occasion is to allow the ancient connection between the prayers of the people and the peace to stand out. Just as those assembled pray for the gift of God's peace to the whole church and to the world, and for people everywhere according to their need, so they share that peace with one another. (Note in this connection the occurrence of the word "peace" at the beginning of forms I, V, and VI of the prayers.) All of this was understood as a part of the people's priestly ministry of reconciliation, focused in the liturgy and lived out day by day.

The Prayer Book specifies no particular gesture or procedure at the exchange of the peace. The original gesture, of course, was a "holy kiss" (Rom. 16:16). It is important to note, however, that the early Christians did not regard it as something bestowed by the clergy on the people. Normally, each worshiper exchanged it with those standing nearby, and it is this practice that is recommended here.

Part C

Of the Eucharistic Liturgy

The eucharistic sacrifice (see BCP p. 859) is offered in obedience to the command of Christ at the Last Supper, "Do this for the remembrance of me." In the early centuries of the church's life, these words were understood as a command to remember and proclaim the life and work of Christ in its totality: his role in creation as God's eternal Word; his incarnation, birth, ministry, death, resurrection, and ascension; and the promise of his coming again in glory.

In the western church during the middle ages, unfortunately, this broad view was gradually narrowed—and the eucharist eventually came to be thought of as the memorial of Christ's death only. Many even came to the belief that it was a sacramental reenactment of Christ's death, and that the priest at the altar personally offered the sacrificed body and blood to the Father on behalf of the assembled worshipers.

To this view, with its outright denial of the teaching of Scripture that the sacrifice of Christ was offered once and for all by Christ himself on Calvary (Heb. 10:12-14), the Protestant Reformers took exception. This, however, did not make their eucharistic theologies any less Passion-centered. The Communion Service of the English Books of Common Prayer of 1552 and 1662, for example, concentrates almost exclusively on Christ's death. The only specific recallings of his resurrection and ascension occur in the Nicene Creed and in the collects and proper prefaces for Easter and Ascension Day.

Within Anglicanism, the movement to recover the fullness of the ancient understanding of the eucharist began in the tiny Scottish Episcopal Church, which (among other things) restored to its prayer of consecration specific mention of the resurrection and ascension. This example was followed in the first American Prayer Book, adopted in 1789, which likewise made mention of these two saving events in its eucharistic prayer. (This same prayer appears in the 1979 Prayer Book as Eucharistic Prayer I.)

Originally, following the pattern known from descriptions of the Last Supper (Luke 22:19-20; 1 Cor. 11:23-25), the eucharist was celebrated in the context of a meal. It involved seven basic actions: (1) bread was taken, (2) a prayer of blessing was said over it, (3) the bread was broken, (4) the bread was shared; then, after a common meal, (5) a cup of wine and water was taken, (6) a prayer of thanksgiving was chanted over it, and (7) all drank from the cup. Early in Christian history, however, the meal (which still survives in the form of church suppers) was separated from the sacramental actions which alone constitute the Lord's memorial. The seven actions were then combined into the four we know today: (1) bread and wine are taken together, (2) a prayer of thanks is offered over them both, (3) the bread is broken, and (4) the bread and wine are shared.

Of the four actions, two stand out as "major events" in themselves: the eucharistic prayer and the reception of communion. The other two have the nature of practical preliminaries: the bread and wine are taken and placed on the altar in order that the eucharistic prayer may be offered over them; the bread is broken (and additional chalices filled) in preparation for the administration of communion.

Because the elements used at the liturgy were, in the early centuries, taken from the bread and wine offered by members of the congregation, the first of the four actions came to be known as the offertory.

1. Of the Offertory Sentences

Offertory sentences first appeared in the Prayer Book of 1549, where they served as a substitute for the variable offertory anthem which formerly occupied this place in the service. In American Prayer Books before 1928, the expectation of the rubrics was that the priest would read as many of the sentences as were needed to cover the whole time of gathering the money offerings of the people.

Since that time, the custom of singing an offertory anthem (or a hymn) has been recovered, one effect of which is to make the use of an offertory sentence redundant. The present Prayer Book has therefore greatly reduced the number of sentences, printed them as an appendix to the rite, and made their use optional.

It is recommended here that there be no offertory sentence at services at which a hymn, psalm, or anthem is sung at this point. It is frequently the organist who is in the best position to judge the amount of time needed for the exchange of the peace, and a cue from the priest in the form of a sentence is not needed. At services without music, especially when there is no usher or server present, the use of the bidding "Let us with gladness . . .," or a selected sentence, may serve as a cue to a member of the congregation to bring the offerings forward. Even then, however, it may not be needed.

It should be noted that the rubrics do not envision the use of a sentence at the time the offerings are placed on the altar (BCP pp. 361 and 376).

2. Of the Preparation of the Table

The spreading of the corporal, and the bringing of the vessels to the altar, are functions of the deacon. In the absence of a deacon, these tasks are appropriately assigned to an adult acolyte. If the number of vessels to be brought to the altar later (at the time of the breaking of the bread) is large, a second corporal may be spread to the right of the principal one.

The recommendation of the Prayer Book is that only one chalice be placed on the altar at the offertory (p. 407). Additional wine, if needed, is to be consecrated in a flagon or cruet. It is also desirable that there be only one paten, and that it be large enough to hold all the bread to be consecrated.

Anciently, and still in the east, the paten and chalice were placed on the altar side by side, which, at celebrations facing the people, allows them both to be seen. The chalice is placed to the right of the paten, so that it is close to the deacon, who stands to the right of the priest. The practice has been restored in the Roman rite, and is recommended here.

3. Of the Bread and Wine

Anglicanism has faithfully adhered to the tradition of the undivided church that the bread to be used at communion be made from wheat flour and that the wine be made from grapes. The bread may be leavened or unleavened.

Since the use of a single loaf of bread is obviously a more powerful symbol of the "one bread" spoken of in the New Testament (1 Cor. 10:17), it is the practice recommended here. When wafer bread is used, it is recommended that large whole-wheat ones be used exclusively, each being broken (at the proper time) into several pieces. If, at very large services, individual wafers are preferred, it is suggested that three or four large ones be consecrated as well, so that all may see a significant amount of bread being broken.

4. Of the Presentation of the Offerings

In the early centuries, the offerings of the people were made in kind. Each person brought an offering of bread and wine (and sometimes other gifts as well) to the service. In many western churches, these offerings were received at the time we call the "offertory." As much of the bread and wine as would be needed for communion was placed on the altar by the deacon or deacons. The remainder was put in a convenient place until after the service, at which time it was portioned out to serve the needs of the clergy and the poor.

In the eastern churches, the offerings were received in a sacristy, or at a table near the entrance of the church, before the service began. After exchanging the peace, the deacons went to the sacristy or table, from which they then returned, bearing the communion vessels with the bread and wine already in them, to the altar. In later centuries, this "transfer of the gifts" became an elaborate ecclesiastical procession, preceded by a lighted candle and accompanied by incense.

As a careful look at the rubrics will show, it is not the intention of the Prayer Book to introduce a "transfer of the gifts" of the eastern kind (p. 361). The intention, rather, is to underscore the fact that the bread and wine are offerings of the people, products both of nature (of which we are God's appointed stewards) and of human labor.

The ceremonial suggested in this book is therefore wholly practical and functional: representative lay members of the congregation bring forward the bread and wine at the same time as others bring forward the money and other gifts. The use of torches, cross, and incense are specifically not recommended, since they tend to attract attention to themselves and away from the persons bearing the gifts.

The rubrics of previous editions of the Book of Common Prayer clearly specified that the money offerings were to be presented before the bread and wine were placed on the altar. The present rubric is less clear, and some have supposed that the order of the words in the rubric, "bread and wine, and money or other gifts," are the order in which they are to be presented. This, however, was not the intent of those who wrote the rubric, who simply intended to mention first the offerings required at every celebration, the "bread and wine," and then those which may or may not be presented at a given service, the "money or other gifts."

It is suggested here that "other gifts," such as food for the hungry, be presented first, then the money, and then the bread and wine. If, as recommended, the bread presented is a loaf, it may be brought forward on the paten on which it will be consecrated, or in a convenient basket.

The rubrics require that those who bring the offerings forward present them directly to the deacon or priest (BCP p. 361). They are not to be handed to servers who in turn present them to the deacon or priest.

As noted elsewhere in this book, the church's traditional custom was that there be nothing on the altar during the eucharistic sacrifice, apart from what is actually needed. Anglican practice since 1662, however, has made the money offerings an exception to the rule. While the present rubric is somewhat ambiguous (it surely does not mean to require that offerings of cases of food be placed on the altar), the recommendation here is that the money offerings be placed on the altar in accordance with past Anglican practice, but removed to the credence before the eucharistic prayer begins.

5. Of the Placing of the Bread and Wine on the Altar

The rubrics of the present Prayer Book, unlike those of its immediate predecessor, do not prescribe that the priest "offer" and "place" the bread and wine on the altar (BCP 1928, p. 73). Instead, it is the deacon, as servant of the church, who prepares and places on it the bread and wine presented by the people. No mention, it should be noted, is made of their being "offered" before being "placed." The reason for this change is a recovery of the ancient, and biblical, understanding that it is the eucharistic prayer itself—said by the priest in the name of all—that offers the gifts to God.

6. Of Music During the Offertory

The rubrics provide for the singing of a hymn, psalm, or anthem during the offertory (BCP p. 361). The use made of music at this point varies considerably from church to church, and even at different services in the same church. Sometimes the usage varies with the season. The rubrics encompass the following possibilities:

a. The congregation sings a hymn. During it, the money offerings are received and immediately brought forward—along with the bread and wine—to the altar. Should the hymn not be long enough to cover the entire action, the organist plays quietly until shortly before the Sursum corda, or (especially during Lent) silence is observed.

b. As above in "a," except that an anthem is sung in place of a hymn. The people sit until the offerings are carried forward, at which point they stand (even if the anthem is not yet finished).

c. All as in "b," except that the offerings are not carried forward until the anthem is finished. All then stand, and instrumental music is played or silence observed.

d. An antiphon is sung by the choir and/or congregation, and is repeated (in whole or in part) after each verse of a psalm sung by a cantor. The verses used need not be the opening verses of the psalm; a selection of the verses most germane to the occasion may also be used. The singing continues until shortly before the Sursum Corda, or, if preferred, until shortly before the incensation. The people sit while the offerings are received, and then stand when they are carried forward.

e. Instrumental music is played while the money offerings are received, the people being seated. All then stand while the offerings are carried forward, during which time a hymn or anthem is sung.

f. Two pieces of music are sung: an anthem during the receiving of the money offerings, while the people sit; and a hymn, all standing, as the offerings are brought forward.

g. Two pieces of music are sung: a short hymn during the receiving of the offerings, and an anthem while they are brought forward, the people standing throughout.

h. Instrumental music is used in place of a hymn, psalm, or anthem (see BCP p. 14). All sit until the offerings are carried forward.

At services at which only one anthem is to be used, it need not always be sung at the offertory. Many anthem texts are equally suitable for use during communion, and some are more suitable at that point. In some circumstances it may be found more convenient to sing the anthem at communion time, and to sing a psalm or hymn at the offertory.

During the seasons of Advent, Christmas, Lent, and Easter, and on holy days, it is desirable that the texts of offertory hymns, psalms, and anthems relate directly to the season or occasion. It is also suitable that they relate to the proper of the day—although this is not always possible or necessary.

Historically, offertory texts used on "green" Sundays have been of a general nature, and this is a tradition worthy of respect. Some of the hymns included under "Holy Eucharist" are also appropriate for occasional use at the offertory on these Sundays. See *The Hymnal 1982*, nos. 302-306, 313, 315, 319, 321, 324, 335, and 339.

The singing of a doxology or the playing of a fanfare at the presentation of the gifts is not recommended here. While there may have been some justification for the practice in the eucharistic rite of previous Prayer Books, when the offertory was separated from the eucharistic prayer by a whole series of other devotions (prayer for the church, general confession, absolution, and comfortable words), the effect in the present rite is to introduce a false climax. As pointed out above, the offertory is a preparatory action, and not an "event in itself." The singing of a doxology, moreover, tends to overwhelm the Sanctus, which, in our revised liturgy, follows closely upon the offertory.

7. Of a Prayer of Preparation by the Priest

The recovery of the tradition that it is the deacon who is the proper minister of the offertory has resulted in a situation where a number of priests feel a need to "do something" upon their arrival at the altar, before proceeding with the (incensation and) washing of hands and the eucharistic prayer. Part of this may simply be a reaction to change, but it is at least equally possible that it is due to a sound devotional instinct. Many historic liturgies provide a private prayer of preparation to be said silently by the priest at this point.

In this book, two alternative prayers are provided for optional use (see chapter 6). The first, based on the apocryphal Prayer of Azariah, has long been associated with this point in the service, and does not—as many medieval offertory prayers did—anticipate what is to be articulated in the eucharistic prayer. The second, which also appears in a lengthened form in the Prayer Book (p. 834), is also a historic prayer of preparation.

8. Of the Incensation

For generations, the censing of the oblations, altar, ministers, and people took place in profound silence; and the mention of silence in heaven while "the smoke of the incense rose with the prayers of the saints" (Rev. 8:1-4) was invoked as a justification of the practice. While the passage of Scripture cited cannot properly be regarded as requiring silence during the incensation, the practice is devotionally effective, and is recommended here, at least for occasional use.

When incense is used, the priest puts some into the thurible and, without reverencing, censes the offerings and the altar (and cross). The deacon or thurifer then censes the ministers and congregation. For details, see 3.8.

9. Of the Washing of the Priest's Hands

One of our earliest detailed descriptions of the eucharistic rite (fourth century) speaks of the washing of hands before the eucharistic prayer as customary practice. No utilitarian reason, however, is alleged for it. Its purpose is understood as wholly symbolic; it is a sign of the purity of heart with which the priest properly approaches the great thanksgiving.

Such "ritual" hand washings were a customary practice at Jewish meals, but it is not known whether the Christian practice is derived from Judaism or was an independent development.

It is suggested that one of the candlebearers (or another server) perform the ceremony. Approaching the priest with the towel over one arm, the bowl in that hand, and the cruet or pitcher in the other, the server pours water over the priest's hands (not just the fingertips). The priest then takes the towel, dries the hands, and replaces the towel on the server's arm.

While washing the hands, the priest may pray silently or may say the psalm verse suggested (Psalm 51:11) in 6.35.

10. Of the Great Thanksgiving or Eucharistic Prayer

The ancestor of Christian eucharistic prayers is the thanksgiving chanted over a cup of wine at the conclusion of Jewish formal meals. This prayer, over what was called the "cup of blessing" (see 1 Cor. 10:16) was pronounced by one person in the name of all, but only after receiving their express consent—ascertained by their favorable response to a bidding such as "Let us give thanks to the Lord our God."

The content of the Jewish prayer (the text was not a rigidly fixed one in Jesus' time) embraced thanks and praise to God for creating the world and for redeeming Israel and making them his people, and supplication for his continued protection and mercy toward his own. The agreement of those present with what was stated in the prayer was signified by the "Amen" which they said at its conclusion.

Christian eucharistic prayers are characterized by the same basic elements, thanks and praise on the one hand, and supplication on the other. The contents, however, as would be expected, are thoroughly Christian. The primary focus of thanksgiving is God's mighty acts in Christ, by which we are saved and made a covenant people; and the supplications are for the church, especially that, by the power of the Holy Spirit, it may be gathered into unity by participation in the body and blood of the Lord.

The present Prayer Book contains six eucharistic prayers, two for Rite One and four for Rite Two.

Eucharistic Prayer I, as stated earlier, is the prayer adopted in the first American Prayer Book in 1789. Though focused on Christ's suffering and death, it also commemorates his resurrection and ascension.

The other five prayers expand this nucleus to include specific remembrance of creation, of the incarnation of Christ, and of his second coming.

Eucharistic Prayer II is a revised version of Prayer I, altered to include the three elements just mentioned. It is also shorter.

Eucharistic Prayer A is the Rite Two equivalent of Prayer II. It is characteristically Anglican in its emphasis on the cross. It is recommended for use in Lent and on some of the "green" Sundays of the year.

Eucharistic Prayer B places special emphasis on Christ's incarnation, using phraseology drawn from one of the oldest surviving eucharistic prayers (third century). Its use is recommended in the seasons of Advent, Christmas (through 1 Epiphany), and Easter, and on some "green" Sundays.

Eucharistic Prayer C is characterized not only by its emphasis on creation and on the revelation of God in the Old Testament, but by its frequent use of congregational acclamations. It is recommended for use on some of the "green" Sundays of the year.

Eucharistic Prayer D is a version of the ancient *anaphora* of St. Basil, a prayer that exists in a number of recensions. Versions of it are included in the service books of the Greek and Slavic Orthodox Churches, in some of the other eastern churches, in the Roman Catholic Church, the Anglican Church of Canada, and the United Methodist Church. It is thus the most widely authorized eucharistic prayer in the Christian world. It is recommended for use on Maundy Thursday, on some of the Sundays of Easter, on the Sunday within the Octave of Prayer for Christian Unity (January 18 to 25), and on some other occasions within the year.

Like many ancient prayers, Prayer D provides for the insertion of special petitions toward the end of the prayer. It should be noted that what is intended are not prayers for the world (the proper place for which is in the prayers of the people), but for particular Christian believers, whether baptized or seeking baptism. It is thus an appropriate place to mention the names of those to be baptized (or to insert a general petition for those to be baptized) on the Sundays immediately preceding their baptism, to mention the newly baptized on the occasion of their baptism and on the Sunday following, and to remember the newly married at weddings, the newly ordained at ordinations, and the deceased at funerals and memorial services. (Such commemorations do not, it should be noted, take the place of the prayers of the people, and the rubrics do not provide for their omission when this prayer is used.)

Traditionally, bishops who use this prayer do not include their own names in the petition "Remember (*NN.* and) all who minister in your Church," but immediately after it add "Remember me, your unworthy servant."

11. Of Proper Prefaces

Eucharistic Prayers I, II, A, and B provide for the insertion of a proper preface immediately after the fixed opening clause of the prayer.

Variable prefaces became a standard feature of western eucharistic prayers, and some ancient service books provided one for every Sunday and holy day in the year and for many other occasions. Later service books greatly reduced the number used, and assigned them primarily on a seasonal basis.

The present Prayer Book includes twenty-two proper prefaces, and requires the use of one of them (when any of these four prayers are used) on every day in the year except "green" weekdays after Pentecost (pp. 377 and 378).

The first three prefaces celebrate the meaning of Sunday itself, the Lord's Day, as it is understood in Christian tradition. It is the first day of the week, and the weekly memorial of three momentous events in the history of the world which Scripture records as taking place on that day: the creation of light, God's first act in creating the universe (Gen. 1:1-5); the resurrection of Christ on Easter Day (Matt. 28:1-10); and the coming of the Holy Spirit on the Day of Pentecost seven weeks later (Acts 2:1-4). This same understanding of Sunday is also featured in some of our hymns. (See *The Hymnal 1982*, nos. 47, 48, 51, and 52.)

The remaining prefaces are concerned with the seasons of the church year and with certain other occasions.

Of the prefaces for seasons, only Lent is provided with alternatives. The use of the second is recommended on Ash Wednesday and the three days following, the first on the first Sunday in Lent and the two weeks following, and the second from the third Sunday in Lent until Palm Sunday.

12. Of the Sanctus

One of the developments in Christian worship that occurred in the fourth century, when the normal setting of worship changed from private houses to public buildings, was an increase in opportunities for congregational singing. It was in this period that the Sanctus, together with a paragraph leading up to it, found a place in most eucharistic prayers.

The text itself, which derives from Isaiah 6:3, had already been in liturgical use as a part of Jewish morning worship, and it is believed that its use by Christians represents a "borrowing" from Jewish practice. To the basic text, most Christian liturgies added the hosannas and Benedictus qui venit from Matthew 21:9 (quoted from Psalm 118:25-26).

In the Prayer Book, the Sanctus is preceded by the rubric "Celebrant and People," an indication that what is expected is a congregational setting. This is in marked contrast to the rubrics preceding the Gloria in excelsis and Christ our Passover (pp. 356 and 364) where the use of the passive voice makes a choir or congregational setting equally appropriate. It can, of course, be argued that the "Celebrant and People" rubric represents a "norm" rather than a demand, and that the occasional use of a choir setting is an appropriate practice. It is certainly true that the corresponding "Priest and People" rubric of the 1928 Prayer Book (p. 79) was commonly construed in this more generous fashion.

At the same time, it is necessary to point out that many settings of the Latin text of the Sanctus are far too long for use at this point in our liturgy. Their effect is virtually to obliterate the sense that the eucharistic prayer is a single whole from "Lift up your hearts" to the concluding "Amen." (At the time these settings were composed, the music was intended to "cover" the silent recitation by the priest of the whole of the rest of the eucharistic prayer, a brief pause frequently being observed between the Sanctus and Benedictus, at which time the host and chalice were elevated.) The recommendation here is that choir settings of the Sanctus be used only rarely, and only when the setting is relatively brief.

Bowing at the Sanctus is a common Anglican custom, although not a widespread Christian practice. In this book it is left to the priest's discretion. One situation in which it is best not done is when there is no choir and the priest's voice is an important part of the musical leadership. In such circumstances an erect posture is preferable. (Such leadership is also made easier if a copy of the music is inserted in the altar book.) Choir members do not observe this bow even when it is made by others, but keep their eyes fixed on the music and the person directing it.

The rubrics of most of the eucharistic prayers provide that those who desire it may kneel after the Sanctus. To signal them to do so by the ringing of a bell, or by an inserted "Let us pray," is still another way of destroying the perception of the eucharistic prayer as a single whole. In most situations, all that is needed is an occasional reminder, made at the time of the announcements or printed in the service leaflet, that those who desire to kneel should do so quietly and without being told to.

13. Of Manual Acts at the Great Thanksgiving

The rubrics of each of the eucharistic prayers prescribe that the priest either "hold" or "lay a hand" (i.e., touch) the bread and vessel(s) of wine at the words of institution. Of the alternatives given, the first, "hold," is the traditional western practice. It was, and is, also the customary practice at Jewish meals.

The recommendation made here is that the priest hold the bread (or the paten) with both hands, at a convenient height above the altar table, throughout the dominical words concerning it. And similarly, to hold the chalice with both hands, one hand below the bowl and one under the foot, during the words concerning it.

The alternative of touching is recommended for use with any additional vessels. It is further suggested that this be done before picking up the principal vessel. Thus, in the case of the wine, the priest first lays a hand on the flagon(s) with one hand, and then picks up the chalice and holds it until after "do this for the remembrance of me."

It is important to remember that, in the context of the eucharistic prayer, the words of institution are addressed to God and not to the congregation. Any temptation to look at the people during them should therefore be rigorously resisted. The time-honored tradition of fixing one's eyes on the book or on the vessel being held is helpful in this regard.

The purpose of a pall is to protect the chalice from insects, and its use is recommended only when actually needed. When used, it is removed for the words of institution, the invocation of the Holy Spirit, and the concluding doxology of the eucharistic prayer. Once removed, it need not be put on again.

The revised Roman rite has retained the late medieval practices of showing the bread and wine to the people after the words of institution and genuflecting to each of the species—practices that are much regretted by some of the most eminent scholars of that communion. Their objection does not, of course, have to do with the legitimacy of reverencing the sacrament, but to the fact that when done at this point, it tends to imply that the remainder of the prayer is really not necessary, or that it is of secondary importance.

Yet it is usually in the part of the prayer that follows the institution narrative that the meaning of the eucharistic action is most clearly articulated. For American Episcopalians, moreover, the matter is complicated by the fact that most of our eucharistic prayers contain an explicit petition for the consecration of the gifts during this part of the prayer.

The issue is not the endless debate about whether it is the words of institution or the invocation of the Spirit (or both) that is essential to consecration. Behind these medieval theories lies a coherent tradition of consecration and offering effected by a prayer of thanksgiving ratified by the people's "Amen," and it is this tradition that the Prayer Book has sought to recover. It is therefore recommended that there be no reverences made to the elements until the prayer is finished.

The ancient practice of lifting up the bread and cup—the bread by the priest and the cup by the deacon—as a gesture of offering during the concluding doxology of the prayer is recommended here. In the early church, the term "eucharist" was used, not only to describe the rite as a whole and the prayer of thanks said over the gifts, but to describe the gifts themselves. They symbolize and embody the thanks offered over them, and by being identified with the body and blood of Christ they become part of his acceptable sacrifice. It is this understanding that lies behind the ceremony of lifting up the gifts before God during the burst of praise that concludes the prayer.

14. Of Gestures During Particular Eucharistic Prayers

The rubrically required alternative gestures of holding or laying a hand on the oblations have been described in the preceding section, together with the recommended ceremonial at the concluding doxology. This section is concerned with other gestures.

Historically, two gestures of blessing have been used in connection with the invocation of the Holy Spirit: an extension of the hands, palms downward, over the oblations, and the sign of the cross. Roman eucharistic prayers are deliberately worded in a manner that allows the use of both gestures. Our American Episcopal prayers are not, and if the ceremonial is to be kept simple, a choice must be made between them.

In the suggestions that follow, a single sign of the cross is recommended in all cases but one, and, following the precedent of the 1549 Prayer Book, always in connection with the verb "sanctify." In the case of Eucharistic Prayer B, where the invocation is very differently worded, the extension of the hands is recommended instead.

Eucharistic Prayer I

After the words of institution, the priest continues the prayer with hands extended.

At the words "And we most humbly beseech thee," joins the hands. At "bless and sanctify," makes a single sign of the cross over the oblations. Continues the prayer with hands extended.

At "And here we offer and present," joins the hands and bows low. At "humbly beseeching thee," stands erect and extends the hands. At "Jesus Christ" in the same paragraph, joins the hands. At "grace and heavenly benediction" signs the self with the cross, then joins the hands.

At "Although we are unworthy," strikes the breast with the right hand, then continues with hands extended.

At "through Jesus Christ our Lord," joins the hands.

Before beginning "By whom and with whom," lifts up the paten (and chalice).

Eucharistic Prayer II

After the words of institution, the priest continues the prayer with hands extended.

At the words "And we most humbly beseech thee," joins the hands. At "bless and sanctify" makes a single sign of the cross over the oblations. Continues the prayer with hands extended.

At "Jesus Christ" in the next paragraph, joins the hands. At "grace and heavenly benediction," signs the self with the cross. Continues with hands extended.

At "through the same Jesus Christ our Lord," joins the hands.

Before beginning "By whom, and with whom," lifts up the paten (and chalice).

Eucharistic Prayer A

After the words of institution, the priest extends the hands and says, "Therefore we proclaim the mystery of faith."

Then, with hands joined, says the memorial acclamation with the people.

Then, extending the hands, continues the prayer.

At "offer you these gifts," joins the hands.

At "Sanctify them by your Holy Spirit," makes a single sign of the cross over the oblations, then joins the hands.

At "Sanctify us also," makes the sign of the cross on the self, then continues with hands extended.

At "All this we ask," joins the hands.

Before beginning "By him, and with him," lifts up the paten (and chalice).

Eucharistic Prayer B

After the words of institution, the priest extends the hands and says, "Therefore, according to his command, O Father."

Then, with hands still extended, says the memorial acclamation with the people. (In this case the memorial acclamation is also an integral part of the priest's prayer.)

At "this bread and this wine," joins the hands.

Says the sentence beginning "We pray you" with hands outstretched, palms down, thumbs almost touching, over the oblations. Then continues with hands extended.

At "the author of our salvation," joins the hands.

Before beginning "By him, and with him," lifts up the paten (and chalice).

Eucharistic Prayer C

After the Sanctus, the priest continues the prayer with hands extended.

During the words, "bring before you these gifts," joins the hands.

At "Sanctify them by your Holy Spirit," makes a single sign of the cross over the oblations, then joins the hands.

Accompanies the words of institution with the usual manual acts.

Continues the prayer with hands extended.

At "Jesus Christ our great High Priest," joins the hands.

Before continuing "to whom, with you," lifts up the paten (and chalice).

Eucharistic Prayer D

After the words of institution, the priest continues the prayer with hands extended.

Then, with hands joined, says the acclamation "We praise you" with the people.

With hands still joined, bows low and says "Lord we pray . . . and upon these gifts." Then stands erect.

At the words "sanctifying them," makes a single sign of the cross over the oblations, and continues the sentence with hands joined.

At "Grant that all," extends the hands and continues the prayer.

At "through your Son Jesus Christ our Lord," joins the hands.

Before beginning "Through Christ, and with Christ," lifts up the paten (and chalice).

15. Of Reverencing the Sacrament

A reverence to the consecrated species immediately after the eucharistic prayer, in the form of a genuflection or deep bow, is recommended.

Much has been said—but only by Anglicans—about the undesirability of genuflecting when standing behind the altar. It is true, of course, that kneeling behind the altar does not produce an edifying spectacle, but a properly executed genuflection—hands on the altar, body erect, down slow, up faster—looks perfectly good in many situations.

This form of reverence is suggested only for the priest-celebrant. Others at or near the altar bow low.

When preferred, the priest may substitute a deep bow for the genuflection.

16. Of the Lord's Prayer

In its position between the eucharistic prayer and the breaking of the bread, the Lord's Prayer functions both as a climactic extension of the great thanksgiving and as a prayer of preparation for communion.

The church fathers saw in the expression "daily bread" a reference to the eucharist as well as to other foods. The eucharist is "living bread"; it is "food indeed" (John 6:51, 55). And the petition for the forgiveness of sins as we forgive those who sin against us is precisely the correct prayer for those who would approach the altar to receive it. It is, moreover, through the eucharist that we are strengthened to serve God, to hallow God's name in our daily lives, and to work and to pray that God's kingdom may come and God's will be done on earth as it is in heaven.

Of the two translations of the prayer provided in the Prayer Book, the contemporary version is in many ways the more accurate, and it is desirable that congregations be familiar with it. Its use is suggested on some occasions, and the use of the traditional version on others.

It should be noted that, according to the rubric, all are to join in the opening words "Our Father."

It is desirable that those who knelt after the Sanctus be encouraged to stand before joining in this prayer. Until this becomes habitual, and when there are kneeling visitors in the front seats, the deacon might say (or sing) "Let us stand" before the priest begins the introduction to it.

17. Of the Breaking of the Bread

The rubrics require (a) that the bread (whether a loaf or a large wafer) be broken, and (b) that a period of silence be observed (p. 364). What the rubrics do *not* envision is (a) that the period of silence be only as long as it takes to break the bread, and (b) that the broken bread be then held aloft, during or immediately after which the priest exclaims, "Christ our Passover is sacrificed for us."

Shortly after the adoption of the present Prayer Book, it was realized that the rubrics of this part of the service could be misleading, especially when a loaf of bread is used. In some places, the loaf was being broken into several parts before Christ our Passover (or some other anthem) was begun, and in others the major part of the bread breaking was being done in the course of administering it, which frequently resulted in a large amount of it being left over. To clarify matters, a supplementary rubric, describing the traditional practice of the church in the centuries when loaf bread was regularly used, was included in the *Book of Occasional Services* (p. 15). The following description is based on that rubric.

The priest:

a. Takes the loaf, or a large wafer, and, holding it a few inches above the paten (not over the chalice), breaks it in two, and then immediately replaces it on the paten.

b. Stands, with hands joined and with head bowed, for a period of silent prayer. An ancient prayer that may be said silently at this point is included in the Synopsis of Ceremonies (6.50).

c. Assisted as necessary by one or more concelebrating presbyters, breaks the rest of the bread, or other large wafers, into as many pieces as will be needed for communion. During this action, Christ our Passover or some other anthem is sung. At the same time, the deacon brings any needed additional patens and chalices to the altar and fills the chalices. (The Synopsis of Ceremonies includes a brief text which the deacon may say silently at this point.) Having done so, the deacon, if needed, assists with the bread-breaking. In the absence of a deacon, the additional vessels are brought to the altar by a concelebrant, an acolyte, or a lay eucharistic minister.

At services without music, at which only one chalice will be used, and when the bread consists of only one large wafer and the needed number of small ones, the following procedure is recommended.

After the initial breaking of bread and the period of silent prayer (items "a" and "b" above), the priest breaks one or both halves of the large wafer into smaller pieces for communion, while reciting the anthem Christ our Passover.

When preferred, Agnus Dei may be said instead, or one of the brief fraction anthems which do not require a congregational response (*Book of Occasional Services*, p. 18, nos. 11-14, adding "says the Lord" to nos. 12 and 13). Either of the two sentences that comprise anthem no. 2 (BOS p. 15) may also be used in this manner, as may individual sentences from some of the other anthems.

Such texts may be recited from memory, but it is frequently helpful to clip a copy of the one to be used to the appropriate page in the altar book.

In Easter Season, it is customary to add "Alleluia" to the (beginning and) erd of such anthems.

18. Of the Anthem at the Breaking of the Bread

The cue for beginning the singing of the fraction anthem is when the priest, having broken the bread once and prayed in silence, continues the bread-breaking.

The text, Christ our Passover, in the second rubric that follows it (BCP p. 364), is described as an anthem, and it is desirable that it be treated as such, and sung by the congregation or choir, or by a cantor and the people.

It is printed in the Prayer Book in versicle and response form as a convenient usage at services without music (as are the Kyries and Trisagion, BCP p. 356). It may also be sung in this fashion at services where the amount of bread to be broken is small, the first line being sung by the priest or by a cantor.

The practice of using it as a versicle and response to introduce a second anthem is not recommended here.

The *Book of Occasional Services* (pp. 15-18) contains a number of anthem texts appropriate for use at this point, including the Agnus Dei. Musical settings for all of them are available, and a few of them appear in *The Hymnal 1982*. The anthem should be chosen on the basis of the time needed to break the bread, and for its appropriateness to the season or occasion.

Agnus Dei originally consisted of one unvarying sentence: "Agnus Dei, qui tollis peccata mundi, miserere nobis," which was repeated as many times as needed to cover the whole time of the breaking of the bread. The reduction to three repetitions dates from the time of the introduction of unleavened wafer bread, and the change of the ending of the third invocation to "grant us peace" is a later touch.

A number of contemporary settings of the Agnus Dei are intended to be performed in the ancient manner, the text being sung by a cantor or choir and repeated (either entire, or just the words "have mercy on us") by the congregation. This is repeated for as long as necessary, with the ending "grant us peace" saved for the final repetition. The setting at no. S160 in *The Hymnal 1982* can be performed in this manner.

Some through-composed Latin settings of the text are appropriate for use at this point, but others are far too long and are better used during communion. Some Renaissance composers, however, provided music for only one or two repetitions of the text (which in modern editions are usually "expanded" into three), and settings such as these can sometimes provide a highly satisfactory fraction anthem, the text being sung only once (ending, of course, with "miserere nobis" and not "dona nobis pacem").

It should be noted that the use of a fraction anthem—including Christ our Passover—is optional and, when preferred, the entire action of breaking the bread and filling additional cups can take place in silence.

The rubrics do not envision the use of a metrical hymn in place of a fraction anthem.

19. Of the Invitation to Communion

The invitation to communion is the traditional place to show a portion of the consecrated bread to the people, and is the practice recommended here. It is convenient that the particle used be the one the priest will receive in communion, since it will then not be necessary to replace it on the paten (except when the priest is to be communicated by another priest or a bishop).

When there is a deacon present, the particle is held over the paten. In the absence of a deacon, it is held over the chalice.

The shorter form of the invitation is suggested for most occasions, and the longer form in Lent.

In places where it has been the practice to ring a bell at this point, there is no need to discontinue it. (The ringing of a bell at other points within the liturgy is not recommended.)

20. Of the Administration of Communion

The rubrics specify that those who are to administer the sacrament to the people shall first have received it themselves (BCP p. 365).

It is suggested that the deacon say the words of administration quietly before the priest eats the bread and drinks from the cup. The priest then communicates the deacon, who retains the cup after drinking from it. The priest and deacon then communicate others in the chancel, beginning with the lay eucharistic ministers who will assist in the distribution.

It is not necessary for the priest to hand vessels to additional ministers of communion. Indeed, in the case of chalices, it is safer if they pick them up themselves.

As suggested elsewhere in this book, it is helpful if there are two persons ministering the chalice for each person ministering the bread.

When communion is administered at "stations," whether before the altar or at the chancel steps or elsewhere in the church, and loaf bread is being used, it is important to remember that the people need time to chew and swallow the bread before approaching to drink from the cup. The most practical way of giving them this time—and simultaneously avoiding slowing down the distribution—is to station the ministers with the cups at some distance (twelve feet is not too far) from those who administer the bread. Even when unleavened wafer bread is used, it is helpful if the ministers do not stand close together.

In some eastern liturgies it is customary for the minister to speak the communicants' names when delivering the sacrament to them, and the practice is sometimes imitated by Episcopalians. While there can be no reasonable objection to it at small intimate celebrations, where everyone knows everyone else, its use at public services presents two difficulties: (a) if the communicant is not expecting it, it can be perceived as intrusive and therefore distracting, and (b) if it is not done to everyone, a sense of favoritism is created, those known to the minister being singled out for special attention. The practice is not recommended.

Another practice sometimes encountered is the squeezing of the communicant's hand by the minister while placing the bread in it. The intent is doubtless friendly, but in many cases the effect is to startle the communicants, and in the case of those with arthritis, it can cause pain. The practice is wholly without precedent in Christian tradition and has nothing to recommend it.

In some places, it is the practice to bless infants and small children in the course of administering communion. While not suggesting denying a blessing to those who seek one, this author would caution against encouraging the practice, particularly in the light of studies that suggest that small children frequently perceive the laying on of a hand (while others are being fed) as a sign of rejection. What is suggested is that Christian parents be encouraged to prepare their baptized children to be regular communicants at the earliest convenient age.

21. Of Music During Communion

The purpose of music sung during communion is to help the communicants approach the sacrament with faith and devotion, and to express the joy of those being drawn into greater unity with Christ and with one another. To accomplish this purpose well, it is virtually essential that the singing begin immediately after the invitation to communion, "The Gifts of God for the People of God." The singing thus accompanies the communion of those in the chancel and those who (approaching the altar during this time) are to communicate immediately after them.

An obvious implication is that the most suitable time for the choir and instrumentalist(s) to receive communion is after everyone else, or toward the end, or shortly after the piece being sung has ended. Ushers can easily be instructed to interrupt the procession of the people to the altar for long enough to allow the choir to join in it at a convenient point.

During the seasons of Advent, Christmas, Lent, and Easter, and on holy days, it is desirable that the texts of communion hymns and anthems relate directly to the season or occasion. A few seasonal hymns have obvious eucharistic overtones: see, for example, *The Hymnal 1982*, nos. 61, 62, 68, 174, 184-186, and 202. Hymns without such overtones are, however, fully appropriate.

The texts of traditional communion anthems, both in these seasons and at other times, show a remarkable diversity, ranging from meditative texts to ones of pure joy and praise, fervent longing, and expressions of faith or penitence. A number of them take their texts from the gospel of the day, and this is still an effective basis on which to choose from time to time.

In the choice of both hymns and anthems, it is important to remember that the act of communion is both a personal and a communal one. Care needs to be taken not to give undue prominence to one of these aspects over the other.

When there is no choir, it is still sometimes possible to sing a communion hymn. All that is needed is a congregation large enough that some can sustain the singing while others go to and return from the altar. Even in a small congregation, however, it is frequently possible to sing one of the traditional communion psalms. All that is needed is a cantor, and a few people who can be depended on to sing the refrains with confidence. The singing of a psalm is also appropriate in medium and large congregations. When there is a choir, the refrains and/or verses might be sung in harmony.

The traditional method of singing communion psalms is the same as that described above for the psalm after the first reading, except that the refrain is sung after each verse. Only as many verses as are needed are used. If the psalm selected is long, the cantor may select individual verses appropriate to the occasion. When the time approaches for the cantor to receive communion, the psalm (if not ended) is broken off. If desired, the cantor may add Gloria Patri, after which the refrain is repeated for the last time. (For traditional texts, see the Appendix.)

In Easter Season, the canticle "Christ our Passover" (BCP p. 83) can be sung during communion in the same way, the people (and choir) responding with a triple "Alleluia" after each paragraph or after each verse. Alternatively, it may be sung by the choir to an elaborate setting.

When possible, it is best to plan for variety in the music used at communion: anthems being used at times, and psalms and hymns at other times.

22. Of the Consecration of Additional Elements

The rubrics provide that if the amount of consecrated bread or wine (or both) is insufficient for the number of communicants, the priest is to consecrate more, using a form provided for the purpose (BCP p. 408). The intent of the form, as the word "also" indicates, is to include the additional bread or wine with that over which the eucharistic prayer was offered, rather than to effect a "separate" consecration. Such supplementary consecration is to take place at the altar (and not at the credence) and is to be done by the priest-celebrant and not a concelebrating presbyter.

It is not necessary, however, that the form be said loud enough for all to hear, just loud enough for one person standing nearby (such as the deacon, or an acolyte or lay eucharistic minister) to hear it and pronounce the "Amen" at its conclusion. It is also not necessary that the distribution of communion by others be stopped.

It should be noted that the Prayer Book, following what was once the universal tradition of the church, expects that all who communicate at the eucharist will receive bread and wine consecrated at that celebration. It does not anticipate that any will be communicated from the reserved sacrament, or that what remains of the reserved species when a fresh supply is reserved will be used to communicate persons at a subsequent eucharist.

23. Of the Reverent Consumption of What Remains

For directions about reserving the sacrament, see chapter 10.

Anglican Prayer Books since 1662 have specifically required that any consecrated bread and wine not needed for communion be reverently consumed by the priest and other communicants. This action is to be distinguished from the ablutions, or rinsing of the vessels (which is dealt with in 24 below).

The 1662 rubrics, which also appeared in all American editions of the Prayer Book until the present revision, required:

a. That after communion, the vessels containing what remained of the consecrated elements be placed on the altar and covered "with a fair linen cloth" (a "postcommunion veil" or second corporal).

b. That immediately after the blessing, the priest and other communicants should "reverently eat and drink the same."

In the seventeenth century, it has been surmised, this eating and drinking by the priest and such communicants as were needed took place while others were leaving the church. Two factors, however, were to change the situation.

a. A desire on the part of the clergy to be at the church door to greet people as they left.

b. The performance of the ablutions publicly, often in an elaborated form (two or three rinsings of the chalice were common) immediately following the consuming of the remaining consecrated elements.

The result was that the entire congregation remained in their places until the ablutions had been completed.

Partly out of a desire to avoid the delay in departure at the end of the service, and partly under the influence of contemporary Roman Catholic practice, it became increasingly common to consume the remains and take the ablutions immediately after the general communion, while the last of the communicants were returning to their places.

The present Prayer Book specifies that the reverent consuming of what remains of the sacramental species take place "either after the Communion of the people or after the Dismissal" (pp. 408-409). It also mentions the deacon in this connection, and provides for the reservation of any needed portion of it.

The Prayer Book also provides that deacons may "remove the vessels from the Altar, consume the remaining Elements, and cleanse the vessels in some convenient place" (p. 555). The context of this rubric is the rite for the ordination of deacons, but it is generally conceded that it may be applied to other situations as well. Marriages and funerals, and Christmas and Easter eucharists, are frequently—like ordinations—occasions when it is difficult to judge how many of those present will communicate, and the amount of the consecrated species remaining can be too large to be conveniently consumed immediately after communion.

It is specifically to be noted, however, that the rubric describes the deacons as removing the vessels from the altar, which evidently assumes that they have been placed there—in time-honored Anglican fashion—after communion.

There is therefore no rubrical justification for the practice (seen in some places) of ministers of communion, after completing the communion of the people, proceeding directly to the credence and there consuming what remains. Still less is there justification for proceeding directly to the credence and not consuming what remains; but instead, placing the vessels on it, and leaving their contents to be consumed after the service.

One argument adduced in favor of such practices is that consuming the remains facing the people is unedifying. Visually, however, it is not very different from what takes place when the ministers receive communion. Most people, in fact, do not even notice it; they are either engaged in their private devotions or busy singing a hymn.

The following procedures are recommended:

a. After communion, the vessels are returned to the altar and placed on it.

b. If there is a deacon or concelebrating presbyter present, the priest goes to the chair and sits.

c. The deacon or concelebrant, assisted by others as needed, consumes what remains and then immediately takes the vessels to the credence. In the absence of a deacon or concelebrant, the priest, assisted by others as needed, consumes what remains. The acolyte, or if necessary the priest, then takes the vessels to the credence.

Should the amount remaining be too large to be conveniently consumed at the altar, either of the following alternatives is recommended:

a. The vessels are left on the altar on the spread corporal, and covered with a linen veil or second corporal, until after the people have departed. To guard against any possible irreverence, it is wise to arrange that a responsible person, such as a member of the altar guild or an usher, will remain nearby. The deacon or priest, with such others as may be needed, then returns to the altar and consumes the remains.

b. The deacon or concelebrant, assisted as necessary by lay eucharistic ministers, takes the vessels to a chapel or other safe place, such as the sacristy, where the portion remaining can be conveniently consumed after the service, and reverently covers them. In the absence of a deacon or concelebrant, lay eucharistic ministers might appropriately take the vessels to the appointed place.

The position of this writer is that the rubrics discussed in this section are norms; they describe what is ordinarily expected to take place. There are, however, situations in which common sense would suggest exceptions. At a very large service, for example, when there are many ministers of communion, it is frequently best if only the priest and the principal deacon return their vessels to the altar, and that the others proceed to a chapel or the sacristy, and there consume what remains in their vessels.

24. Of the Ablutions

The consuming of the remaining consecrated bread and wine at the altar does not necessitate that the ablutions take place there as well, and it is recommended that they do not.

The following alternatives are suggested:

a. The deacon (or concelebrant) takes the vessels to the credence, rinses them with water, consumes the rinsing, and wipes them with the purificator. A single rinsing is ordinarily sufficient. In the absence of a deacon or concelebrant, the rinsing may be done by an (adult) acolyte or by a lay eucharistic minister.

b. The vessels are taken to the credence, placed on it, and covered with a veil (such as a traditional chalice veil). After the congregation has departed, they are uncovered and rinsed.

25. Of a Hymn After Communion

The rubrics provide that a hymn may be sung before or after the postcommunion prayer (BCP p. 409). This is intended to be the "final" hymn of the service, since the rubrics do not provide for a hymn after the dismissal (see 29 below).

The hymn selected may be related to the season, occasion, or proper of the day, or it may be a general hymn. Some of the hymns included under "Holy Eucharist" are intended specifically for use at this point in the service, and others are as appropriate here as they are during communion. See *The Hymnal 1982*, nos. 300, 312, 326, 334, 336, 340, 341, 344-347.

Hymn 380, which concludes with the familiar doxology, is also appropriate for use at this point.

26. Of the Postcommunion Prayer

The postcommunion prayer is led by the priest either from the chair or from the altar. If led from the altar, the acolyte first places the sacramentary in the center of it (unless, of course, vessels containing the sacrament are occupying that position).

At weddings, ordinations, and burial or memorial services, a proper postcommunion prayer is used instead. These may be said by all together, or by the priest alone, the people responding with "Amen."

27. Of the Blessing

For centuries, the liturgy concluded with the postcommunion prayer and the dismissal. No blessing was given by the priest and none was expected.

The blessing, when it first appeared, was thought of as taking place after the service; and it did, in fact, follow the dismissal. Though popular, and increasingly widespread, the practice was strongly opposed by many liturgical scholars, who believed that such blessings should be given only by bishops. Even by the time of the Protestant Reformation a priestly blessing was not a universal custom.

The first Book of Common Prayer, issued in 1549, required a blessing, but used it as a substitute for the dismissal, which it eliminated completely. This remained the standard Anglican practice for four centuries. The trial use liturgy of 1967 proposed a return to earlier practice. It substituted a dismissal for the blessing, and argued that a blessing after communion was, at best, redundant. Some found this argument compelling, and believed it sufficiently persuasive that omission of the blessing would become a trend as the various Christian communions revised their eucharistic liturgies.

This did not happen. The revised Lutheran and Roman rites, for example, both require a blessing. The present Prayer Book (in Rite Two) permits but does not require one. The recommendation made here is that one be given except in the season of Lent.

The Rite Two Eucharist provides no texts for this blessing. The priest is therefore free to select or even compose one. The Prayer Book does, however, contain texts that are appropriate: the shorter alternative given for Rite One (p. 339), the similar form used at the ordination of priests (p. 535), and the Aaronic blessing (p. 114).

The *Book of Occasional Services* (pp. 20-27) provides blessings appropriate to the seasons of the church year, and their use is here recommended. They need not, it should be noted, be used throughout the season. The one for Advent (preferably the longer form) might be used only on the first Sunday, as a way of marking the beginning of the season. In Easter season, on the other hand, one might choose to use the longer form only on Easter Day and on the following Sunday, and the shorter form on the other Sundays.

When the longer forms are used, it is usually necessary to reproduce them in the service leaflet, so that the people know when to say "Amen." When they are sung, the problem does not arise, since the musical cadence indicates where the Amens belong. (The musical formula for singing blessings is given in the musical appendix to the altar book.)

28. Of a Prayer Over the People

The *Book of Occasional Services* provides a series of prayers for use in Lent in place of a blessing (pp. 22-24).

The tradition of using such prayers is very old and, originally, they were used all year round. They are typically prayers that God will look upon his people (or "family") with mercy, or "graciously behold" them, or help and protect them. They are, in fact, the precursors of our present declaratory blessings.

Traditionally, they are introduced by a diaconal bidding: "Bow down before the Lord." All (except the priest) then kneel or bow low, and the priest, with hands outstretched over them, says the prayer.

The limiting of such prayers to the season of Lent took place only in the west (about the year 600), but it did serve to give a special character to the conclusion of Lenten liturgies. Their use is recommended.

In the case of the numbered prayers, the choice is at the discretion of the priest. They can also be used sequentially, no. 1 being used on Ash Wednesday and on the three days following, no. 2 on the first Sunday in Lent and throughout the week, no. 3 on the second Sunday, etc.

29. Of the Dismissal

In the days before the clergy entered and left the church in procession, the dismissal was a simple matter. The deacon bade the people to depart, and they left. Once the processional exit was established, however, the situation changed. Politeness bade the congregation to wait until the ministers had left. Their own departure was thus delayed, but not for long.

By the end of the middle ages, however, epilogues to the service were common. Sometimes (as noted above) a blessing was "added." Sometimes a "last gospel" (John 1:1-14) was read. Sometimes there was a blessing of the weather, or an anthem in praise of the Virgin. On some occasions, a whole series of devotions ensued. The Roman rite before the Second Vatican Council regularly added the last gospel, and vernacular prayers at the foot of the altar. The sense of the dismissal as a sending out had disappeared.

Anglicans in general, and Episcopalians in particular, however, can claim no superiority in this regard. Though our rites had substituted a blessing for the dismissal (and in 1552 eliminated the processional exit of the clergy), the rubric before the blessing was crystal clear. The priest was to let the people "depart with this Blessing" (BCP 1928, p. 84).

In the decades preceding the present revision of the Prayer Book, they did not then depart. Typically, there followed:

a. The consuming of the remaining bread and wine and the ablutions.

b. A hymn, during which the ministers returned in procession to the sacristy.

c. A prayer in the sacristy, frequently said loud enough to be heard by all and followed by a choral Amen.

d. Soft organ music (and sometimes chimes) while the candles were extinguished, all kneeling.

e. The postlude, which was the signal to depart.

The present Prayer Book, in restoring the dismissal, has also sought to recover its significance as a true sending out. To that end, it repealed the general rubric that permitted a hymn to be sung after the service (BCP 1928, p. viii). The intent is that the people, having responded "Thanks be to God," and witnessed the departure of the ministers, should themselves depart.

The Prayer Book provides four texts for the purpose, three of which speak of going forth. The fourth was sometimes used in the past in the seasons of Advent and Lent. The present rubrics do not limit it to those times, and it is best that it not be used on a seasonal basis. For most occasions, one of the first two are recommended.

The dismissal is said or sung by the deacon, and in the absence of a deacon by the priest (not by a concelebrant).

It is as the People of God, and as members of Christ's Body, that the congregation goes forth. Their ministry in the world is a ministry of reconciliation (2 Cor. 5:18). But this ministry does not begin at the church door, it begins with baptism, and with the liturgy itself. There, refreshed by the word of God, God's people offer their prayers for the church, and for the world to which they are sent. Then, their sins forgiven, and with hearts raised on high, they recall with thanks God's mighty deeds, are united with

Christ in his sacrifice, strengthened in their union with Christ and one another, given a foretaste of the heavenly banquet (BCP p. 859-60), and sent forth in Christ's name.

But they are not sent forth into a world where Christ is absent. It is God's world, and in it Christ awaits them. They go forth to "seek and serve Christ in all persons," loving their neighbors as themselves, to "strive for justice and peace among all people, and respect the dignity of every human being" (BCP p. 305). In these ways, also, they worship God.

6

Synopsis Of Ceremonies

The pages that follow provide a synopsis of the ceremonies recommended in this book for principal celebrations of the Holy Eucharist in parish churches. Alternatives to some of the suggestions will be found under the heading "The Service in Detail" (5.A–5.C).

For services at which Rite One is used, see also 3.9.

For recommendations about other celebrations, see chapter 8, "Celebrations with Small Congregations."

This synopsis provides for, as a norm, the participation of one priest, a deacon, two readers, an adult acolyte, lay eucharistic ministers (when needed), two candlebearers, and (if desired) a thurifer. Provision is made, however, by the use of sections in italics, for situations in which the services of a deacon or adult acolyte (or both) may not be available.

For ceremonial directions for concelebrating presybters, see 2.2.

The Priest	**The Deacon**
1. Vests in alb, stole, and chasuble.	1. Vests in alb and stole (and dalmatic).
2. If incense is used at the entrance, puts incense into the censer before the procession begins.	2. If not holding the gospel book, assists at the putting on of incense by holding the boat.
3. Enters the church in procession during the singing of a hymn or other music.	3. Enters the church in procession. If bearing the gospel book, precedes the priest (and any concelebrating presbyters), holding the book high for all to see. On arrival before the altar, makes no reverence, but immediately places the book on it (closed and lying flat and with the opening to the left), then moves to the right to be out of the way of the (concelebrants and) priest when they reverence the altar. If not bearing the gospel book, walks to the right or left of the priest. *In the absence of a deacon, a concelebrant may bear the gospel book.*
4. Reverences the altar with a deep bow. If the sacrament is reserved in the chancel, may genuflect instead.	4. If not bearing the gospel book, reverences the altar with the priest, bowing low or genuflecting as the priest does.
5. Where it is the custom, kisses the altar (simultaneously with the deacon).	5. Where it is the custom, joins the priest in kissing the altar.

The Acolyte	**Other Ministers**
1. Vests in alb or cassock and surplice.	1. Vest in alb or cassock and surplice.
2. Takes the processional cross.	2. The candlebearers take their candles or torches. If incense is used, the thurifer takes the thurible to the priest, who puts on incense.
3. Carries the cross in the procession. On arrival before the altar, pauses briefly, and, without reverencing, puts the cross in the accustomed place. Then stands aside, and out of the way, until the priest goes to the chair.	3. Enter the church in the accustomed order. If incense is used, the thurifer leads. The candlebearers accompany or, when the way is narrow, precede the cross. On arrival before the altar, they pause briefly, and then, without reverencing, put their candles in the places appointed and go to their seats.
	In the absence of a deacon, a vested reader may bear the gospel book.
	4. Others in the procession reverence the altar in the accustomed manner (a low bow or genuflection) and go to their places. If the altar is not to be censed, the thurifer puts the thurible in its place or takes it to the sacristy.

The Priest	**The Deacon**
6. If incense has been used at the entrance, may cense the altar while walking around it.	6. If the priest censes the altar, stands aside, facing it.
7. Proceeds to the chair.	7. Goes to the seat at the priest's right, and stands with hands joined.
	In the absence of an acolyte, holds the sacramentary while the priest reads from it, both at this point and at other times when it is needed.
8. Making the sign of the cross, begins the appointed opening acclamation and, if it is to be used, says the collect for purity with hands extended.	8. Makes the sign of the cross at the opening acclamation.
9. In Easter Season, may sprinkle those present with water as a reminder of their baptism (see 5.A.7).	9. If there is to be a ceremony of sprinkling, presents the vessel of water with the sprinkler to the priest, and, afterwards, returns them to their place.
10. Remains standing at the chair, with hands joined, during the singing (or recitation) of the Gloria in excelsis, the Kyrie eleison, or the Trisagion.	10. Remains standing, with hands joined, during the singing (or recitation) of the Gloria in excelsis, the Kyrie eleison, or the Trisagion.
11. With hands extended toward the people, greets them with the words "The Lord be with you." After their reply, says "Let us pray" with hands joined, and pauses for a moment of silent prayer.	

The Acolyte	Other Ministers
	6. If the altar is to be censed, the thurifer hands the censer to the priest, and, after the censing, puts it in its place or takes it to the sacristy.
7. Takes the sacramentary (altar book) and opens it to the correct page. Then, holding the book open with both hands, so that the opening will be toward the priest, goes and stands in front of, but a little to the left of, the priest.	7. Remain standing, joining in the responses, and in the music sung by the congregation, until after the collect of the day. They then sit for the reading of the lessons and the psalm.
8. Remains holding the book while the priest says the opening acclamation (and collect for purity). Does not make the sign of the cross while holding the book.	8. Make the sign of the cross at the opening acclamation.
	9. *In the absence of a deacon, one of the candlebearers presents the vessel of water with the sprinkler to the priest.*
10. Stands aside during the singing of the Gloria in excelsis, Kyrie eleison, or Trisagion (but remains in place if the text is recited rather than sung).	

The Priest	**The Deacon**
12. Says the collect of the day with hands extended.	12. Remains standing for the collect.
13. Sits during the reading of the lessons and the psalm.	13. Sits during the reading of the lessons and the psalm.

The Acolyte	Other Ministers

12. Holds the sacramentary, open to the proper page, before the priest for the collect of the day.

13. Sits during the reading of the lessons and the psalm. Except when there are two deacons present, may occupy the seat at the priest's left.	13. The appointed reader goes to the lectern-pulpit, and announces and reads the first lesson. After the reading (after "Thanks be to God") remains standing in place, without looking at the congregation, during the period of silence that follows. Then, unless appointed to lead the psalm, returns to place.

14. If the psalm is to be sung responsorially, it is led by a cantor standing at the lectern-pulpit. Immediately after the last repetition of the refrain, the cantor returns to place.

If the psalm is to be recited, rather than sung, it is announced and led, from the lectern-pulpit, by the reader of the first lesson.

If the psalm is sung by the choir or by all, without refrain, the choir may stand, but the ministers and people remain seated.

15. The appointed reader goes to the lectern-pulpit and reads the second lesson in the manner described in 13 above.

The Priest	The Deacon
16. If a hymn is sung after the second reading, stands, and joins in the singing up to the point where the preparations for the gospel procession are to be made.	16. If a hymn is sung after the second reading, stands, and joins in the singing up to the point where the preparations for the gospel procession are to be made.
17. If incense is to be used at the gospel, puts incense into the censer.	17. If incense is to be used at the gospel, assists the priest by holding the boat.
18. Blesses the deacon, either by making the sign of the cross or laying hands on the deacon's head, and quietly saying one of the following forms or other suitable words: a. The Lord be in your heart and on your lips that you may worthily proclaim his gospel: In the Name of the Father, and of the Son, and of the Holy Spirit. b. May the Spirit of the Lord be upon you as you announce the good news to the poor. Remains standing at the chair, with hands joined, and faces the lectern-pulpit during the reading of the gospel.	18. Stands before the priest, and, bowing low, asks for a blessing. After receiving the blessing, responds "Amen."
19. *In the absence of a deacon, the gospel is read by a concelebrating or assisting presbyter, if one is present, or by the priest. The priest who is to*	19. Goes before the altar and bows low. Then reverently takes up the gospel book. Preceded by the

The Acolyte	Other Ministers
16. If a hymn is sung after the second reading, stands and joins in the singing.	16. If a hymn is sung after the second reading, all stand and join in the singing.
17. If incense is put on, receives the boat from the deacon (or priest) and returns it to the credence.	17. If incense is to be used at the gospel, the thurifer takes the censer and boat and goes to the priest. After incense is put on, goes to the place where the gospel procession will form.
	18. The candlebearers take their candles and go before the altar, taking care to allow enough room for the deacon or priest to approach it to pick up the book.
19. During the reading of the gospel, stands, with hands joined, facing the deacon or priest who	19. If an alleluia or tract is sung during the gospel procession, it is led by the cantor from a suitable place, or sung by the choir. The

The Priest	The Deacon

read it goes before the altar and, bowing low, quietly says the following or similar words:

Cleanse my heart and my lips, Almighty God, that I may worthily proclaim your holy gospel.

Then, taking the gospel book from the altar, and preceded by the (thurifer and) candlebearers, goes to the lectern-pulpit. Meanwhile, an alleluia or tract may be sung. The gospel is announced and read as described in item 20 in the deacon's column.

20. Makes the sign of the cross on the forehead, lips, and breast at the announcement of the gospel.

(thurifer and) candlebearers, goes to the lectern-pulpit. Meanwhile, an alleluia or tract may be sung.

20. At the lectern-pulpit, places the book on the desk, opens it, and announces the gospel, making the sign of the cross with the right thumb on the book and then on the forehead, lips, and breast. If incense is used, censes the book with three swings before reading the text.

At the end of the reading, adds "The Gospel of the Lord" (and, where it is the custom, kisses the book).

Closes the book and, in accordance with local preference, returns it to the altar, leaves it on the lectern, places it on a shelf within the pulpit, or takes it to the credence.

The Acolyte	**Other Ministers**
reads it. (The processional cross is not used at the gospel.) If, however, the reader of the gospel is also to be the preacher, the acolyte may participate in the gospel procession in order to be in a convenient place to receive the gospel book after the reading and take it to the credence or return it to the altar.	procession goes in the following order: (thurifer), candlebearers, (acolyte), deacon or priest. On arrival at the pulpit-lectern, the candlebearers stand on either side of it, or on the floor facing it (but far enough apart so as not to impede the congregation's view). The thurifer stands nearby. All face the reader of the gospel.
20. Makes the sign of the cross on the forehead, lips, and breast at the announcement of the gospel.	20. All, except the candlebearers, make the sign of the cross on the forehead, lips, and breast at the announcement of the gospel. If incense is used, the thurifer then hands the thurible to the deacon or priest, who censes the book and returns the thurible. The thurifer then steps away a few paces and stands facing the deacon or priest during the reading. After the reading, the candlebearers return their candles to the customary place. The thurifer puts the censer away or takes it to the sacristy.

The Priest	**The Deacon**
21. Normally preaches the sermon.	21. On occasion, preaches the sermon. Otherwise, sits in the accustomed place during it.
22. When it is to be used, begins the Nicene Creed (unless the opening words are to be intoned by a cantor or sung by all). Bows the head at the name of Jesus and bows low at "By the power . . . and was made man." Keeps the hands joined throughout.	22. Joins in the recitation of the creed, when it is used. Bows the head at the name of Jesus, and bows low at "By the power . . . and was made man."
23. Standing at the entrance to the chancel, or other convenient place, makes such announcements as are pertinent to the occasion and to the intercessions which are to follow. May introduce the prayers with a sentence of invitation related to the occasion, the season, or the proper of the day. Asks the people to stand.	23. Where it is customary, or where the priest prefers it, makes the announcements.
24. Stands at the chair, with hands joined, while the deacon or some other person reads the names and leads the prayers.	24. Standing at the lectern-pulpit, or in the midst of the congregation, or in some other convenient place, reads the lists of names and concerns to be prayed for, and invites the congregation to offer additional intentions, either silently or aloud (see 5.B.11).
25. Says the collect at the end of the prayers with hands extended.	25. Ordinarily leads the prayers of the people.

The Acolyte	**Other Ministers**
21. Sits for the sermon.	21. All sit for the sermon.
22. Holds the sacramentary before the priest during the recitation of the creed. Bows the head at the name of Jesus, but does not bow low when holding the book.	22. Facing the altar, join in the recitation of the creed, when it is used. Bow the head at the name of Jesus, and bow low at "By the power . . . and was made man."
	24. *In the absence of a deacon, or when preferred, a lay person appointed reads the list of names and concerns to be prayed for, and invites the congregation to offer additional intentions, either silently or aloud.*
25. Holds the sacramentary before the priest during the collect that concludes the prayers.	25. *In the absence of a deacon, or when preferred, a lay person leads the prayers of the people.*

The Priest

The Deacon

26. *In the absence of a deacon, bids and leads the confession of sin, if it is to be said.*

Bows low, with hands joined, for the confession of sin.

26. If the confession of sin is to be said, remains standing and, with hands joined, says, "Let us confess our sins against God and our neighbor."

After observing a moment of silence, bows low and leads the confession of sin. (If leading the confession from the midst of the congregation, may kneel.)

27. Begins the absolution with hands joined, makes a single sign of the cross over the people at the words "forgive you all your sins," and concludes the form with hands joined.

27. Makes the sign of the cross at the absolution.

28. With hands extended toward the people, says "The peace of the Lord be always with you." After their reply, exchanges the peace with the deacon and other ministers and, as appropriate, some of the members of the congregation.

28. Exchanges the peace with the priest, acolyte, and others as appropriate.

29. After the peace, sits while the table is prepared. (If a hymn is sung at this point, may stand and join in the singing.)

In the absence of a deacon, the vessels and corporal are brought to the altar and arranged by the acolyte, or in the absence of an acolyte by a concelebrating pres-

29. Removes the gospel book from the altar (if it is there). Brings the vessels to the altar. Spreads the corporal and places the chalice and paten on it (unless the bread is to be brought forward on the paten), with the chalice to the right of the paten. Removes the purificator from the chalice and places it on the altar to the right of the corporal. Places the

The Acolyte	**Other Ministers**
26. If the confession of sin is used, holds the book for the (deacon and) priest during the confession and absolution.	26. Bow low or kneel for the confession of sin.
27. Does not make the sign of the cross at the absolution if holding the book.	27. Make the sign of the cross at the absolution.
28. Exchanges the peace with the priest and deacon, and with others as appropriate.	28. Exchange the peace with the priest, deacon, and others as appropriate.
29. Sits or stands until needed to assist the deacon.	29. Stand and join in the singing if a hymn is sung. Otherwise sit until after the offerings are brought forward, then stand.
In the absence of a deacon, removes the gospel book from the altar, brings the vessels to the altar, spreads the corporal, and arranges the vessels as described in item 29 in the deacon's column.	

The Priest	The Deacon
byter. If necessary, however, the priest performs these functions as described in item 29 in the deacon's column.	pall (if used) to the right of the purificator. Returns the burse and veil, if either are used, to the credence.
	Stands aside, or sits, until the offerings are brought forward.
30–31. *In the absence of a deacon, a concelebrating presbyter (if one is present) receives the offerings of the people and places the gifts on the altar as described in the deacon's column. Otherwise, the priest performs these functions.*	30. Standing in front of the altar, at the center, and facing the people, receives the offerings presented by the representatives of the congregation in the following order:
	i. Any special gifts, such as offerings of food for the hungry. These the deacon receives and hands to the acolyte, who puts them in a suitable place.
	ii. Money offerings. The deacon receives the plate or plates with the money and, without elevating them, hands them to the acolyte who places them on the altar.
	iii. Bread and wine. If only two vessels are presented, the deacon receives the bread box (or paten with the bread) with one hand and the flagon or cruet containing the wine with the other, and, after bowing to the presenters, proceeds behind the altar and places the offerings on it, off the corporal. If more than two vessels are

The Acolyte	**Other Ministers**
30. Stands to the right of the deacon (or priest if no deacon is present) and assists by receiving such gifts as are handed over by the deacon or priest and taking them to their proper place, as follows:	30. *In the absence of an acolyte, or when needed, one or both of the candlebearers assist the deacon or priest in receiving the gifts.*
i. Special gifts, such as offerings of food. Takes and puts them in a convenient place, but not on the altar.	
ii. Money offerings. Places them on the altar at one of the corners.	
iii. Bread and wine (unless carried to the altar by the deacon). Places them on the altar, off the corporal.	

The Priest	The Deacon
	presented, or if it is more convenient, the deacon may hand one or some of them to the acolyte, or an additional server, to bring to the altar. 30a. If preferred, the deacon may stand behind the altar, at the center, to receive the offerings of money, bread, and wine. In such cases the representatives of the congregation come directly to the altar and hand the offerings across it. The deacon receives them and, without elevating them, hands the money offerings to the acolyte, and places the bread and wine on the altar, off the corporal. 31. Standing behind the altar, at the center, puts the bread on the paten (if it was not brought forward on the paten) and pours the wine into the chalice. If additional bread or wine is needed, notifies the acolyte, who brings it from the credence. Adds a little water to the chalice (and to the flagon if additional wine is to be consecrated). Arranges the vessels on the corporal so that the chalice is to the right of the paten, and the flagon (if used) is to the right of the chalice, but further back on the corporal. If there are insects about, covers the chalice with a pall or folded corporal.

The Acolyte	Other Ministers
30a. Stands to the right of the deacon (or priest if no deacon is present). Receives the money offerings from the deacon or priest and places them on a corner of the altar.	
31. If additional bread or wine is needed, brings it to the altar. Brings the water cruet (without the stopper) to the altar and presents it to the deacon or priest. Returns the water cruet to the credence. Takes any other cruets or vessels which are not needed at the altar to the credence.	31. *When necessary, one of the candlebearers assists the deacon or priest by performing the functions described in item 31 in the acolyte's column.*

The Priest	The Deacon
32. Goes to the altar. Without touching the vessels, bows low and, with hands joined, prays silently, using one of the following forms or other suitable words:	32. Moves to the right, and steps back a few steps, to allow the priest to come to the center of the altar.

    a. In a humble spirit and with a contrite heart, let us be accepted by you, O Lord, and so let our sacrifice be in your sight this day, that it may be pleasing to you, O Lord our God.

    b. Be present, be present, O Jesus our great High Priest, as you were present with your disciples, and be known to us in the breaking of bread.

The Priest	The Deacon
33. If incense is used, puts incense into the censer and censes the oblations and the altar (and the cross). Is then censed by the deacon or thurifer. See 3.8.	33. If incense is used, assists the priest by holding the boat. After the incensation of the altar, takes the thurible and censes the ministers and people (unless it is preferred that the thurifer do this).

The Acolyte	**Other Ministers**

32. Remains near the credence.

33. If incense is used at the offertory, the thurifer brings the censer and boat to the priest. After incense is put on, hands the censer to the priest and takes the boat to the credence.

In the absence of a deacon, or when preferred, the thurifer censes the ministers and people.

After the censings, returns the thurible to its place or takes it to the sacristy. Alternatively, may remain in the chancel, swinging the censer very gently during the eucharistic prayer.

The Priest	The Deacon
	34. Removes the alms from the altar and places them on the credence.
35. Goes to the corner of the altar for the washing of hands, and may say silently: Create in me a clean heart, O God, and renew a right spirit within me.	
36. Returns to the center of the altar. Is joined at the altar by the concelebrating presbyters, if any are present.	36. *In the absence of an acolyte, brings the sacramentary to the altar, and puts it in place.*
37. With hands extended toward the people, says "The Lord be with you." At "Lift up your hearts," raises the hands. Says "Let us give thanks . . ." with hands extended.	37. Stands to the priest's right, a few steps back, and with hands joined, from the beginning of the great thanksgiving until just before the doxology to the prayer. *In the absence of an acolyte, may cross over behind the priest to assist at the book if this is needed or desired.*
38. Says the preface with hands extended.	
39. Joins the hands (and may bow) at "Holy, holy, holy Lord." If the bow is observed, stands erect at the first "Hosanna in the highest."	39. Bows at "Holy, holy, holy Lord" if the priest does.

The Acolyte	Other Ministers
34. *In the absence of a deacon, takes the alms from the altar and places them on the credence.*	34. *In the absence of both a deacon and an acolyte, one of the candlebearers takes the alms to the credence.*
	35. One of the candlebearers takes the lavabo bowl, water cruet (without stopper), and towel, and goes to the priest for the washing of hands. Returns to the credence.
36. Brings the sacramentary, with its stand or cushion (if used), to the altar, and places it to the priest's left.	36. *In the absence of both a deacon and an acolyte, one of the candlebearers brings the sacramentary to the altar.*
37. Stands aside in a convenient place, facing the altar and with hands joined, from the beginning of the great thanksgiving until the invitation to communion.	37. Remain standing at their appointed places, facing the altar, and with hands joined, from the beginning of the great thanksgiving until the invitation to communion.
But if it is desired that the acolyte turn pages for the priest, stands to the priest's left, a few steps back. Steps forward to turn pages as needed, then immediately steps back.	
39. Bows at "Holy, holy, holy Lord" if the priest does.	39. Bow at "Holy, holy, holy Lord" if the priest does.

The Priest	The Deacon
40. Continues the prayer with hands extended.	
(For gestures appropriate to Prayer C, see 5.C.14.)	
41. Begins the institution narrative with hands joined.	
42. At the words "He took bread," takes up the loaf, or the paten, with both hands. (If there is a second vessel of bread, lays a hand on it briefly and then takes up the loaf or paten with both hands.) Holds the loaf or paten at a convenient height (about 8 inches) above the table until after the words "Do this for the remembrance of me." Then replaces it on the corporal.	
43. If a pall is used, removes it (or the deacon may do this.) See 5.C.13.	43. If the chalice is covered with a pall, removes it (unless the priest prefers to do so).
44. At the words "He took the cup," takes the chalice with both hands. (If there is also a flagon or cruet of wine to be consecrated, lays a hand on it briefly, then takes up the chalice.) Holds the chalice at a convenient height above the table until after the words "Do this for the remembrance of me." Then replaces it on the corporal.	

The Acolyte   **Other Ministers**

The Priest	**The Deacon**
45. Continues the prayer with the gestures appropriate to the particular prayer (see 5.C.14).	
46. At the beginning of the doxology which concludes the prayer, takes the paten with both hands and, lifting it up in a gesture of offering, says the doxology. After the people have responded "Amen," replaces it on the corporal.	46. At the beginning of the doxology which concludes the prayer, steps forward to the altar and lifts up the chalice while the priest lifts up the paten. After the people have responded "Amen," replaces it on the corporal. Steps back to place.
In the absence of a deacon, takes the paten in one hand and the chalice in the other, and lifts them up at the doxology.	
47. Reverences the sacrament with a genuflection or low bow.	47. Reverences the sacrament with a low bow.
48. Says the invitation to the Lord's Prayer with hands joined. Then, with hands extended, joins the people in saying the prayer.	48. Joins in the Lord's Prayer with hands joined.
49. Takes the loaf (or large wafer) and breaks it over the paten. Then immediately (and without elevating it) replaces it on the paten.	
50. Stands, with hands joined and with head bowed, and prays silently, using the following or other words:	

As grain that was scattered on
plains and on hillsides was
gathered and made one loaf, so

The Acolyte	Other Ministers
47. Reverences the sacrament with a low bow.	47. Reverence the sacrament with a low bow.
48. Joins in the Lord's Prayer with hands joined.	48. Join in the Lord's Prayer with hands joined.

The Priest	The Deacon
gather your Church from the ends of the earth into your kingdom. Glory to you, O God, for ever.	
51. Assisted by one or more concelebrating presbyters, if any are present (or, if necessary, by the deacon), breaks the loaf into as many pieces as will be needed for communion. If wafer bread is used, breaks several large wafers so that at least some (and preferably all) of the communicants will receive a piece of broken bread. *In the absence of a deacon or concelebrating presbyter, fills any additional chalices which have been brought to the altar.* In the meantime, the anthem "Christ our Passover" or "Lamb of God" or some other anthem may be sung. *At services without music, may begin the recitation of "Christ our Passover" or "Lamb of God."*	51. Brings any needed additional patens and chalices (with their purificators) to the altar. Fills the chalice(s) from the flagon or cruet. If needed, assists in the breaking of bread. After filling the additional cup(s) or, if only one cup is used, after the initial breaking of the bread, may say silently: Wisdom has built her house, she has mixed her wine, she has set her table. Glory to you, O God, for ever.
52. Holding a portion of the broken bread over the paten with the thumb and forefinger of one hand, and lifting up the paten with the other, says the invitation to communion, "The Gifts of God for the People of God."	52. Lifts up the chalice, while the priest lifts up the paten, at the invitation to communion.

The Acolyte	Other Ministers
51. *In the absence of a deacon or concelebrating presbyter, brings any needed additional chalices and patens to the altar.*	51. *If necessary, a lay eucharistic minister brings any needed patens and chalices to the altar.*
	52. Immediately after the invitation to communion, "The Gifts of God . . . " the lay eucharistic ministers go to their places near the altar where they will receive communion. Others go to where they will be communicated.

The Priest	**The Deacon**
In the absence of a deacon, holds a portion of the consecrated bread over the chalice and lifts it up while saying the invitation to communion.	
53. Replaces the paten (or chalice) on the corporal.	53. Replaces the chalice on the corporal.
54. Continues to hold the particle of bread while the deacon says the words of administration quietly. Responds "Amen" and communicates.	54. Remains at the priest's side, and quietly speaks the words of administration for the bread and cup at the priest's communion.
Takes the chalice and holds it while the deacon says the words of administration. Responds "Amen" and drinks from the cup.	

In the absence of a deacon, may say these words quietly:
    The Body of our Lord Jesus Christ
    keep me in everlasting life.
    The Blood of our Lord Jesus Christ
    keep me in everlasting life.

But if there are one or more concelebrating presbyters, the priest receives communion from one of them in this manner: The priest steps to the left to allow the concelebrant to come to the center of the altar. The concelebrant then communicates the priest, saying the usual words of administration. The priest in turn communicates the con-

The Acolyte   **Other Ministers**

The Priest	The Deacon

celebrant. They then communi- cate any other concelebrants and the deacon or deacons (see 2.2).

55. Communicates those who are to assist in the distribution.

55. Receives communion from the priest, standing, and retains the chalice. Administers the cup to any lay ministers of communion.

56. Takes the paten and goes to the people. Before each communicant, takes a portion of the bread and, holding it above the paten, says the words of administration. Then (after the person has responded "Amen") places it in the communicant's hand.

56. Ordinarily administers the chalice, holding it before each person while saying the words of administration, and allowing the communicant to respond "Amen" before drinking from it.

If preferred, administers the bread while lay ministers of communion administer the cup.

57. After administering communion, returns to the altar, places the paten on it, and returns to the chair and sits. (If a hymn is sung, may stand and join in the singing.)

In the absence of a deacon or concelebrating presbyter, consumes the remaining bread and wine, assisted as necessary by the acolyte and other ministers of communion. (For directions about reserving the sacrament, see chapter 10.) But if the amount remaining is too large to be immediately consumed, leaves the vessels containing the sacrament

57. After administering communion, returns to the altar, places the chalice (or paten) on it, and then, assisted as necessary by the acolyte and lay eucharistic ministers, consumes the remaining bread and wine. (For directions about reserving the sacrament, see chapter 10.) But if the amount remaining is too large to be immediately consumed, either (a) leaves the vessels containing the sacrament on the altar (on the corporal), covering them with a veil or second corporal, until after the people have left, or (b) takes the vessel or vessels to a

The Acolyte	**Other Ministers**
55. Receives communion standing.	55. Receive communion standing.
56. If licensed to do so, may assist in administering the sacrament.	56. Taking their vessels, the lay eucharistic ministers proceed to communicate the people, always allowing them to say "Amen" before receiving. (See 2.7 and 4.2)
57. If needed, assists in consuming the remaining bread and wine.	57. After administering the sacrament, the ministers of communion return to the altar and place their vessels on it. If needed, they assist in consuming the remaining bread and wine. They then return to their places.

The Priest	The Deacon

on the altar (on the corporal), covering them with a linen veil or second corporal, until after the people have left.

chapel or other safe place where the portion remaining can conveniently be consumed after the service, and reverently covers them.

58. If there is no other minister who can do so, takes the empty vessels to the credence and either (a) proceeds immediately to rinse the vessels and consume the rinsings or (b) covers them with a veil and leaves them there to be rinsed after the people have left.

58. Takes the empty vessels to the credence (assisted by the acolyte) and either (a) proceeds immediately to rinse the vessels and consume the rinsings or (b) covers them with a veil and leaves them there to be rinsed after the people have left.

59. Standing at the altar, or at the chair, says "Let us pray" with hands joined. Then, with hands extended, leads the people in the recitation of the postcommunion prayer.

59. Stands at the priest's right, at the altar or at the chair, with hands joined, during the postcommunion prayer.

60. If a short blessing is to be used, begins it with hands joined. Makes the sign of the cross over the people at the mention of the Trinity.

60. Makes the sign of the cross in the usual way if the priest blesses the people.

The Acolyte	Other Ministers

58. Assists, as needed, in taking vessels to the credence. If the vessels are to be cleansed immediately, ministers the water. Returns to the altar, folds the corporal, and takes it to the credence.

In the absence of a deacon or concelebrating presbyter, takes the vessels to the credence and either (a) rinses them and consumes the rinsings or (b) covers them with a veil and leaves them there to be rinsed after the people have left. Folds the corporal and takes it to the credence.

59. If the postcommunion prayer is to be said at the altar, places the sacramentary in the center of it. If the prayer is to be said at the chair, takes the book and holds it before the priest for the prayer and for the blessing.

59. Stand, with hands joined, for the postcommunion prayer.

60. If a blessing is given, makes the sign of the cross (unless holding the book).

60. If a blessing is given, make the sign of the cross.

The Priest	**The Deacon**
If one of the longer seasonal blessings from the *Book of Occasional Services* is used, recites it with hands outstretched, palms down, over the people. At the trinitarian blessing, joins the hands, and then makes the sign of the cross in the usual way.	
In Lent, if a prayer over the people is used, recites it with hands outstretched over the people. The sign of the cross is not used with these prayers.	In Lent, if a prayer over the people is used, introduces it by saying, with hands joined: "Bow down before the Lord."
In the absence of a deacon, says "Bow down before the Lord" before beginning the prayer over the people.	
61. *In the absence of a deacon, says the dismissal with hands joined.*	61. Says the dismissal with hands joined.
62. Where it is the custom, kisses the altar.	62. Kisses the altar if the priest does.
63. Standing before the altar, makes the customary reverence (a low bow or genuflection) with the deacon and other ministers, and departs in procession.	63. Standing before the altar, to the right or left of the priest, reverences the altar with the priest. Walks beside the priest in the procession out.

The Acolyte   **Other Ministers**

61. Immediately after the dismissal, takes the processional cross and goes before the altar. Stands before it, facing it, far enough away to allow the procession to form in between the cross and the altar.

61. Immediately after the dismissal, the candlebearers take their candles or torches and go to stand on either side of the crossbearer. Others go to their proper places in the procession.

63. As soon as the priest has reverenced the altar, turns and leads the procession out.

63. Reverence the altar with the priest (except for the candlebearers, who do not reverence) and depart in procession.

7

The Holy Eucharist with Baptism

The normal occasion for the administration of Holy Baptism is, in the words of the Book of Common Prayer, "within the Eucharist as the chief service on a Sunday or other feast" (p. 298). It is, moreover, recommended that—to the extent possible—baptisms be reserved for the Easter Vigil, the Day of Pentecost, All Saints' Day or the Sunday following, the Feast of the Baptism of the Lord (1 Epiphany), and occasions when a bishop is present.

In some churches it may be necessary to appoint one or two other Sundays as regular occasions for baptism, one perhaps in summer and the other in early autumn. Whenever possible, however, baptisms should not be scheduled in the season of Lent.

When baptism is administered at a principal service, the liturgical color for the entire service is that of the day. The collect, readings, and psalm are those also appointed for the day. But should it happen that none of the appointed readings relates to baptism, the priest may substitute one or more (one is usually sufficient) of those appointed at no. 10 on page 928 of the Prayer Book (see BCP p. 312, 6th rubric). This provision does not, however, apply to the seven principal feasts; on these days the appointed proper must be used without alteration even when baptism is administered at a separate service (BCP p. 18, conclusion of last rubric).

When baptism is administered at a separate service at other times, the color is white, and the collect, psalm, and readings are those appointed for baptism (BCP pp. 203 or 254 and 928).

When baptism is administered within the eucharist, the chasuble is properly worn throughout the service. (If, for any reason, the eucharist is not celebrated, the use of a cope is appropriate.)

In most Episcopal churches the font or baptistry is located at some distance from the chancel, frequently at the other end of the building. It is this arrangement which is presupposed in the ceremonial directions given below. In them the candidates and sponsors gather at the chancel steps or in the chancel itself for the presentation and examination of the candidates and the baptismal covenant, go in procession to the font for the thanksgiving over the water and the act of baptism, and then return to the chancel for the prayer over the candidates and the laying on of hands and anointing.

Alternatively, the presentation of the candidates may take place at the font. In this case, the ministers proceed to the font after the sermon, and the candidates and sponsors join them there. The procession to the chancel for the prayer over the candidates and what follows is still appropriate, however, and is recommended here.

In some churches and chapels, the font is located in the chancel itself or just outside it, usually on the side of the church opposite the pulpit. Where this is the case, the formal processions mentioned in the detailed description given below would be omitted. Instead, the ministers, candidates, and sponsors move to the font for the thanksgiving over the water in an informal yet orderly way and, after the baptisms, return to their former places.

1. Of Preparations for the Service

The following are placed in readiness on a table near the font:

a. A ewer or other vessel filled with water, to be poured into the font at the appropriate time; unless, in the ancient fashion, the baptizing is to take place in "living" water (see 1.6 above).

b. A baptismal shell or other vessel for use during the baptismal act (unless the baptisms are to take place by immersion).

c. A sufficient number of towels.

d. Candles to be distributed to the newly baptized (if the custom is observed).

e. White garments for the newly baptized (if the baptisms are by immersion or total affusion).

f. A vat and sprinkler (if it is customary to sprinkle the congregation with baptismal water).

If chrism is to be used, the following are placed on the credence:

a. A vessel of chrism or an oil stock containing it.

b. A bowl containing warm water with a little liquid detergent and a hand towel (or a plate with a piece of lemon and slice of bread) for cleansing the priest's hand after the anointing.

If the font is large, it is expedient for it to be partially filled before the service begins. The remainder of the water is then added at the appropriate point in the service. If the water is very cold, it is suitable to warm it somewhat by adding hot water.

The paschal candle (which, outside of Easter season, is appropriately placed near the font) is lighted before the service begins.

2. Of Baptism by Immersion or Total Affusion

The baptism of infants by immersion was the customary practice in England both before and after the Reformation, and fonts were made large for that express purpose. It is also the method of baptism listed first in the Prayer Book (p. 307).

When using this method, it is customary to dip the child into the water three times while pronouncing the traditional formula. There is precedent, however, for immersing the baby's head only at the last dipping, the minister taking care to cover the child's mouth with one hand and to pinch the nostrils closed while doing so. Immediately following the baptism, the child is handed to a parent or godparent who stands waiting with towels to wrap it in. Then, at a convenient table nearby, the child is diapered and clad in a white robe. If infants are to be immersed at a service at which adults and older children are to be baptized by affusion (pouring), it is convenient to baptize the adults and older children first.

The baptism of adults and older children by immersion—which was the normal practice for centuries—first took place in a separate baptistry because it involved total nudity. Today, when it is customary that such candidates be partially clothed (usually in swimwear), such privacy is not a necessity. It is necessary, however, that there be a place (folding screens can be used, but a more permanent arrangement is desirable) where the candidates can disrobe before being baptized and dry themselves off and be clothed afterwards. It is helpful if such candidates are instructed to wear clothing that can be removed easily and quickly.

When baptizing such candidates, the minister stands or kneels at the edge of the pool, and places a hand on the person's head during each of the three immersions, while at the same time pronouncing the baptismal formula. The ancient practice was for the candidate to bow forward into the water, thus signifying assent.

An alternative to immersion which also has its roots in ancient practice is total affusion. In this practice, the candidate stands or kneels in a shallow pool. The minister, taking up water from the pool in a suitable vessel three times, pours it over the person's head each time while reciting the traditional formula.

(Affusion is also an alternative to immersion in the case of infants. The child is placed in the font in a sitting position, and water is taken up and poured over the head.)

Immediately after being baptized, each candidate is given a towel (by a server), dries the head, and proceeds to the place prepared, where he or she finishes drying off and, after putting on such undergarments as desired, is clothed in a white robe.

Since the dressing of the candidates can take some time, it is appropriate that, immediately after the last of them has been baptized, a suitable psalm, such as Psalm 32, or a hymn be sung. Psalm 23 is also appropriate, unless it is to be sung during the procession to the chancel.

3. Of the Service Through the Baptismal Covenant

a. The rite begins as prescribed for celebrations of the Holy Eucharist. See the "Synopsis of Ceremonies" (5.A.1-4).

b. In place of the collect for purity, the appointed versicles are said by the priest with hands joined (BCP p. 299).

c. Gloria in excelsis may then be sung (rubric, p. 312).

d. The salutation and collect follow, after which the service continues as usual until the end of the sermon.

e. After the sermon, the priest takes a Prayer Book, goes to the front of the altar or to the chancel steps, and stands facing the people. The deacon, the candlebearers (without their candles), and the acolyte stand nearby. (If the thanksgiving over the water is to be sung, the acolyte holds the sacramentary, closed, but marked at the proper page.)

f. The candidates and their sponsors come forward and stand facing the priest. It is helpful if they stand to the right and left of center, so that the congregation can also see the priest. The priest then says, "The Candidate(s) for Holy Baptism will now be presented."

g. The adults and older children to be baptized are then presented, one at a time. After each presentation the priest asks, "Do you desire to be baptized?"

h. The infants and younger children are then presented, one at a time. The questioning of the parents and godparents, however, is done once for all.

i. The priest continues the rite with the renunciations, the question addressed to the congregation, and the commitment to the baptismal covenant.

4. From the Prayers for the Candidates to the End

a. Immediately after the invitation to prayer for the candidates, a procession is formed and goes to the font in the following order:

1. (In Easter Season only) the deacon or a server bearing the paschal candle.

2. The candlebearers (without candles).

3. The acolyte.

4. The priest (and deacon if not bearing the paschal candle).

5. The candidates with their sponsors.

In the meantime, the deacon or a person appointed sings or says the petitions for the candidates (BCP p. 305).

b. Alternatively, the procession may go to the font during the singing of Psalm 42 or some other psalm or a hymn. See the appendix (15.1) for a suggested text. In this case, the invitation to prayer and the petitions for the candidates are not said until the procession has arrived at the font.

c. On arrival at the font, the priest takes a position behind it, facing the people (when this is possible). Others take positions in such a way that the congregation can see what is taking place.

d. The priest says the prayer that concludes the petitions, the Prayer Book or sacramentary being held by the acolyte.

e. Unless water is already running in the font, one of the candlebearers fills the font with water or pours additional water into the font or pool.

f. The priest begins the thanksgiving over the water with the usual gestures, and says or sings the prayer with hands extended. At the point specified, the priest touches the water (or traces the sign of the cross in it with one hand) and then concludes the prayer with hands extended. (It should be noted that the ceremony of lowering the paschal candle into the water is only used at the Easter Vigil.)

If the water is in a pool, the priest kneels on one knee, if necessary, in order to touch the water.

g. The sponsors then present each candidate—by speaking the person's name aloud—to the priest, or to an assisting priest or deacon, who then immerses or pours water on the head of each candidate three times while saying the baptismal formula.

h. If the baptisms have been by immersion or total affusion, a psalm or hymn may be sung while the candidates are clothed in their baptismal robes. See the appendix (15.1) for suggested texts.

i. The deacon or a server may then hand a lighted candle, lit from the paschal candle, to each of the newly baptized. In the case of infants and younger children, the candle is handed to a godparent.

j. The procession then returns to the chancel in the same order in which it came.

k. Where, however, it is customary to sprinkle the congregation with baptismal water, one of the candlebearers first fills the vat with water from the font or pool, puts the sprinkler (which may be a sprig of evergreen) into the vat and hands it to the priest. Then, as the procession returns, the priest sprinkles the people, alternately sprinkling those to the right and to the left. In the meantime, Psalm 23 or one of the anthems suggested in the appendix may be sung.

l. On arrival in the chancel, the priest (gives up the sprinkler and vat and) stands facing the congregation. The candidates stand facing the priest. The acolyte holds the book for the priest.

m. With hands outstretched, palms down, over the candidates, the priest says the appointed prayer over them.

n. Then, if chrism is to be used, the deacon or a server brings the vessel or oil stock containing it and stands at the priest's side.

o. The candidates come before the priest one by one, the adults and older children standing or kneeling, or the priest may go to them for the laying on of hands and anointing. A sponsor may place a hand on each candidate's shoulder during this action.

p. The laying on of hands and anointing are done in one of the following ways:

1. The priest takes the vessel of chrism, pours a small amount of it into the palm of the right hand, places the hand against the person's forehead, and spreads the chrism across the forehead (and, if desired, down the person's cheeks) while reciting the words, "*N.*, you are sealed by the Holy Spirit in Baptism." Then, while saying the words, "and marked as Christ's own for ever," the priest traces a cross on the person's forehead with the thumb.

2. The priest dips the right thumb into the chrism or touches the oil stock with it. Then, laying the hand on the person's head, traces a cross on the forehead with the thumb while saying the prescribed formula.

q. A server then brings the bowl of warm water and the towel (or the plate with lemon and bread) to the priest, who uses them to remove the oil from the hand.

r. Then, invited by the priest, all join in welcoming the newly baptized.

s. The newly baptized then extinguish their candles (except at the Easter Vigil).

t. The peace follows, at which time the priest kisses the infants and exchanges the peace with the other newly baptized persons before greeting anyone else.

u. The service then continues with the announcements, the reading of names, and the prayers of the people, for which the brief form given in the appendix (15.3) may be used. (The Prayer Book permits the omission of the prayers of the people, but it is suggested that this is not appropriate at principal services.)

v. The confession of sin is omitted.

w. The eucharist continues with the offertory.

Except on the seven principal feasts, the proper preface of baptism may be used.

The newly baptized (and their sponsors) appropriately receive communion before other members of the congregation. Where it is the practice to communicate infants on the occasion of their baptism, this is suitably done under the species of wine alone. The priest or deacon may either use a small spoon or touch the wine with a finger and put it to the child's mouth. Alternatively, the administration of communion may be done by a parent, using the second suggested method.

8

Celebrations with Small Congregations

There are times and circumstances when, because the congregation is small or the space about the altar is limited, the eucharist is celebrated with fewer ministers than are recommended in this book for principal celebrations. Chief among these are weekday and early Sunday morning celebrations, which frequently take place in a chapel. The suggestions that follow assume that the priest is assisted by a single server. Directions are also given for situations in which there is no server.

In some chapels it is possible to have a free-standing altar, but seldom is it possible for the priest's chair to be behind it. The ceremonial directions in this chapter therefore assume that the chair will be on one side of the chancel (preferably the side opposite the lectern), facing across, or partially turned toward the people.

In other cases, space does not permit a free-standing altar. In many instances, what happens when the altar is brought forward is that a chapel that was a comfortable and pleasing place in which to worship is changed into one in which it is awkward to minister. When this is true, it is better that the altar be left against the wall, but that the priest preside at the liturgy of the word from the chair, and only go to the altar at the time of the offertory.

It is desirable that the chapel have an attractive lectern (not merely a movable stand) for the reading and preaching of the word of God.

To the extent possible, the norms of participation by various orders and ministers should be followed. For example:

a. Lay members of the congregation (unvested) read the lesson(s) that precede the gospel, announce and lead the psalm, and lead the prayers of the people. They also bring the gifts to the altar at the offertory.

b. If the server is an adult, he or she brings the vessels to the altar at the offertory, assists with the chalice (if licensed and needed), and takes the vessels to the credence after communion. If there is no other lay person present who can do so, the server also performs the duties listed above under "a."

c. A deacon, when present, fulfills the normal duties of that ministry. If there is no lay person present who is prepared to read the lesson(s) before the gospel and lead the psalm, the deacon performs these duties as well.

1. Of Preparations for the Service

a. The credence is prepared as usual. Only if the credence is too small are the vessels placed on the altar. In that case, the corporal is spread beforehand. The cushion or bookstand may also be placed on the altar, in the position it will occupy during the eucharistic prayer.

b. The bread and wine to be brought forward are put in a convenient place. If, however, there is no one who can be asked to bring them up, they are placed on the credence.

c. The lectionary, or a Bible, properly marked, is placed on the lectern. (At small services, it is usually more convenient not to use a separate gospel book.)

d. If there is not a server or deacon present who can hold the sacramentary for the priest, the best solution is to place a simple, portable lectern in front of the priest's chair. This will be found more convenient than a kneeling desk, since it will hold the book at a convenient height for praying with hands extended.

e. The candles are lighted.

2. Of the Service Itself

a. Preceded by the server, the priest enters the chapel or church. They reverence the altar together (or genuflect if the sacrament is present) and go to their places.

b. The priest begins the service in the usual way.

c. After the collect of the day, if there is no one else prepared to do so, the priest goes to the lectern, reads the lesson(s), and leads the psalm.

d. After the lesson(s) and psalm (if read by someone else), the priest goes before the altar, bows low and says the prayer "Cleanse my heart," then goes to the lectern and reads the gospel. If already at the lectern, however, the priest does not go before the altar but, instead, simply turns to face the altar, bows in place to say the prayer, then turns back to the lectern and reads the gospel.

e. The service continues as appointed until after the peace.

f. At the offertory the priest brings the vessels to the altar, or uncovers them if they are already there, and receives the gifts of the people in the usual way. The server brings the sacramentary to the altar.

g. If there is no server, however, the following procedure may be used instead. The priest places the sacramentary on the altar, takes the corporal to the altar and spreads it, then receives the gifts of the people and takes them to the credence. At the credence the priest puts the bread on the paten and pours the wine and water into the chalice. Then, holding the paten in one hand and the chalice in the other, the priest goes to the altar and places them on the corporal. The same procedure may appropriately be used when the bread and wine are already on the credence and there is no server.

h. If there is no server, the priest (after praying silently before the altar) goes to the credence for the washing of hands. This is most easily done by pouring water into the lavabo bowl, and then dipping the hands into it.

i. The service continues as usual with the Sursum corda dialogue, preface, and Sanctus. As pointed out above (3.3), it is suitable to sing this part of the liturgy (or at least the Sanctus) even if there is no other music at the service. If standing with back to the people, the priest turns to face them for the opening dialogue. Similarly, the priest, holding the bread and cup, faces the people for the invitation to communion, "The Gifts of God. . . ."

j. After communion, the priest consumes the remaining bread and wine at the altar, then takes the vessels to the credence and rinses or covers them. If the credence is too small, however, the priest may either leave the vessels on the corporal and cover them (in which case the rinsing will take place after the people leave) or rinse them at the altar.

k. If standing with back to the people during the postcommunion prayer, the priest turns and faces them for the blessing and dismissal.

9

Of Holy Communion
After the Liturgy

The following suggestions are intended for situations in which those who provide child care during the eucharist would otherwise be deprived of an opportunity to receive Holy Communion that day. In every case, it is desirable that such persons be communicated from bread and wine consecrated at that eucharist.

One of the happy results of liturgical reform is the willingness to admit children to communion at a much younger age than was long customary. In some places, children become regular communicants from the day of their baptism. In others, communion is given at baptism, but not again until a few years have passed. At any rate, practice varies widely, as is to be expected in a period when the church seeks viable ways of including youngsters in the eucharistic fellowship.

In some places, children, including infants, are present for the entire liturgy, and child care is not provided. In others, children of school age have their own liturgy of the word (or a church school class) and join the adults in the church at the offertory. In some places, infants and toddlers are brought in, or fetched, at the time of communion. In others, child care is provided throughout the service, with the result that some adults cannot be present when communion is being administered.

The following procedure is recommended for the communion of such persons:

1. After the general communion, a paten and chalice with a sufficient amount of consecrated bread and wine is left on the altar, on the spread corporal. These vessels are then covered with a linen veil or second corporal. Any empty vessels are taken to the credence.

2. The liturgy concludes in the usual way, except that a genuflection is substituted for the usual bow to the altar.

3. The candles at the altar are not extinguished. (If the only lights at the altar are torches or candles which were carried in at the entrance, they are left at the altar. Those who carried them walk immediately behind the cross during the procession out.)

4. To prevent any possible irreverence, a server, usher, member of the altar guild, or other responsible person, remains near the chancel until the congregation has departed and those to be communicated have arrived.

5. A priest or deacon (vested as for the liturgy, or in alb or surplice with stole) then enters the chancel, genuflects, goes to the altar, and uncovers the vessels.

6. Communion is then administered, using the form for Communion under Special Circumstances (BCP p. 396). (This form is also included in the loose-leaf altar book, but not in the bound edition.)

7. On most occasions, it is suitable to begin with one of the four passages of Scripture printed in the rite, and then to continue with "Let us pray," a brief period of silent prayer, the collect, the confession of sin (if desired), and what follows.

8. On the principal feasts, it would be more appropriate to begin with a Scripture reading proper to the day; for example, the appointed gospel on Christmas and Easter, and the reading from Acts on Ascension Day and Pentecost.

9. After communion, the remaining bread and wine are consumed, and the rite concludes with one of the usual postcommunion prayers and a blessing or dismissal, or both.

In some churches it may be preferable to communicate such persons in an adjacent chapel.

Where this is the case:

a. Before the eucharist, a corporal is spread on the chapel altar. A Prayer Book, lectionary or Bible (if needed), and a linen veil or second corporal are placed in readiness.

b. After the general communion, a deacon or lay eucharistic minister takes the paten and chalice containing the consecrated elements to the chapel, places them on the corporal, covers them with the veil, and lights the candles.

c. To guard against any irreverence, a responsible person remains in the chapel until the communicants arrive.

d. The rite takes place as described in 9.5–9 above.

10

Of the Reservation of
the Sacrament

The Prayer Book provides for the reservation of the consecrated sacrament for three purposes:

1. For the communion of individuals who cannot be present at a public celebration of the eucharist.

2. For the communion of a congregation in the absence of a priest. (See chapter 11.)

3. For communion on Good Friday, from the sacrament consecrated at the Maundy Thursday liturgy.

The practice of the early church was that all assembled for the eucharist should communicate from bread and wine consecrated at that service. But so strong was the sense of "one bread, one body" (1 Cor. 10:17) that it was felt necessary that those prevented from being present should also be communicated from the sacrament consecrated at the service; and in our earliest description of the Sunday service (second century) it is the deacons who perform this ministry.

The rubrics of the rite for the ordination of deacons make specific mention of this practice (p. 555), and in 1985 the canons were amended to provide that lay eucharistic ministers, supervised, when possible, by a deacon, might take the sacrament to those unable to be present directly following the celebration.

Anciently, such communions—for reasons of convenience—were frequently administered under the form of bread only, and it may be noted that neither the rite for Communion under Special Circumstances (BCP p. 396) nor the canons specifically mention both kinds. Where one kind is the norm, however, it is all the more important that the Prayer Book requirement that priests celebrate the eucharist with such communicants on a periodic basis be scrupulously observed. This will provide them times for receiving in both kinds, as well as opportunities to participate in the entire eucharistic action.

The following directions pertain to communion in both kinds. Where only one kind is to be reserved, the references to wine should be passed over.

If there is only one vessel containing wine to be consecrated and reserved, it may be placed on the altar at the offertory.

A preferable procedure, however, and especially when there is more than one such vessel, would be to fill them from the same flagon or cruet used to fill any extra chalices used in the distribution, as described below.

After the general communion, the lay minister(s) appointed come to the altar, bringing with them the vessels to be used in their ministration. The deacon (or a priest) puts a sufficient amount of the consecrated bread into the pyx(es), and pours enough consecrated wine into the vessel(s) for wine. Bearing the sacrament, the eucharistic ministers depart, either immediately or after the dismissal. They may suitably be accompanied by friends of those to be communicated.

But if the number of lay ministers is large, and the service would be unduly prolonged, or if it is desired that the eucharistic ministers should have the opportunity to greet their fellow parishioners after the service (and receive greetings to be conveyed to those to be communicated), the following order may be observed:

After the general communion, the deacon, or a lay eucharistic minister assisting in the distribution, takes the flagon and a paten with a sufficient amount of bread and puts them in the aumbry (or on a spread corporal in a locked cupboard in the sacristy). Then, at an agreed time following the service, the lay ministers gather with the deacon (or a priest) at the place of reservation for the filling of the vessels, and then depart.

It is desirable that those to be so communicated be prayed for by name at the service, and not merely included in the list of those who are sick.

In many churches, the sacrament is continuously reserved, both for scheduled communions of the sick and shut-in by the clergy on weekdays, and for use in emergencies. Such reservation properly takes place in a secure, locked aumbry or tabernacle, the key to which is kept in a place where it is accessible only to those who will need to use it. It is customary that a lamp of clear glass burn continuously nearby.

In some cases, the reservation is of bread only, and in others, of both kinds. Both practices can claim ancient precedent.

It is strongly recommended that the bread to be reserved not be consecrated in a ciborium. The Prayer Book prefers that there be only one chalice on the altar during the eucharistic prayer, and ciboria look too much like chalices not to cause visual confusion. It is therefore suggested that the empty ciborium be placed in readiness on the credence, and not brought to the altar until after the general communion, at which time the bread is put in it, and the vessel taken by the deacon or a lay minister of communion to the place of reservation.

Similarly, if there is a flagon of wine on the altar for filling other chalices, and the same flagon is not to be used for reserving the wine, it is preferable that the vessel for reservation be brought to the altar after communion and filled.

The amount of bread and wine reserved should not exceed what may reasonably be expected to be needed, and this supply should be renewed on a periodic basis. This is especially true of the wine, which spoils easily.

The most convenient way of doing this is to own two sets of vessels for reservation. The set containing the freshly consecrated species having been placed in the aumbry after communion, the other set can then be removed, the contents reverently consumed, and the vessels cleansed, either immediately, or after the service.

When the sacrament is reserved at a service at which there is no deacon or lay eucharistic minister, and the aumbry is not nearby, the priest leaves the vessels containing the reserved sacrament on the altar (on the spread corporal) until after the dismissal. Then, having reverenced the sacrament, takes the vessels containing it and, without reverencing the altar, proceeds to the place of reservation.

11

Of Holy Communion by a Deacon

The directions in this chapter pertain to services at which—in the absence of a bishop or priest—a deacon is to preside at the liturgy of the word and, with the bishop's express authorization, administer communion from the reserved sacrament (BCP p. 408). Such a service is sometimes described as a "deacon's mass." It is more appropriately called "The Liturgy of the Presanctified" or "Liturgy of the Word and Holy Communion."

Since, in such circumstances, there is no possibility of a supplementary consecration, the amount of bread and wine consecrated and reserved for such a service should be sufficient for the largest number of people who may reasonably be expected to be present.

The directions which follow assume that the consecrated bread is in a ciborium or other suitable vessel and that the wine is in a flagon or cruet. (If the bread is to be administered from the vessel in which it is reserved, the references to the paten given below should be ignored.)

1. Of Preparations for the Service

a. If there is an aumbry or tabernacle in the chapel or church, the sacrament is reserved there. Before the service the key is placed on a corner of the altar.

b. If there is no aumbry or tabernacle, or if it is more convenient, the sacrament is reserved in the sacristy. In a suitable place there, a corporal is spread, and the vessels containing the sacrament are placed on it and covered with a linen veil or second corporal.

c. The chalice, purificator, paten, corporal, cruet of water, and any other needed patens and chalices (with purificators) are placed in readiness on the credence.

d. The sacramentary is marked and put in its place near the chair. Since the introduction to the Lord's Prayer (BCP p. 408) differs from that ordinarily used, it is helpful (unless the deacon has memorized it) to clip a copy of it to the page on which the prayer occurs.

e. The deacon vests in alb and stole and, if desired, dalmatic. Others vest as usual.

2. Of the Service Itself

a. The procession enters in the usual way, the deacon bearing the gospel book. If incense is used at the entrance, the deacon puts some into the censer before the procession begins.

b. On arrival at the altar, the deacon places the book on it, and may kiss and/or cense it. Then, standing at the chair which would otherwise be used by the priest, the deacon begins the liturgy, the acolyte holding the sacramentary in the accustomed manner. (When praying collects and greeting the people, the deacon uses the same gestures a priest would use.)

c. At the preparations for the gospel procession, the deacon puts on incense (if it is to be used), goes before the altar and says secretly the prayer "Cleanse my heart" (6.19), and takes the gospel book. The gospel and what follows take place as usual.

d. At the absolution, the deacon substitutes "us" for "you" and "our" for "your."

e. After the peace, while the money offerings are being collected, the deacon spreads the corporal, and places the paten(s) and chalice(s), not on the corporal, but to the right of it. The acolyte then places the sacramentary (on its cushion or stand) to the left of the corporal as usual.

f. The deacon receives the money offerings and places them on the altar. The acolyte then takes them to the credence.

g. Then (after the hymn or anthem, if one is being sung) the deacon explains to the people what is to happen next. In very few instances will all present know about communion from the reserved sacrament; a few selected sentences of explanation will therefore almost always be needed.

h. A communion hymn is then sung. Hymns suitable for this point in the service are numbers 302, 303, 307, 308, 309, 314, 318, 319, 321, 323, 329, 331, 335, and 339 from *The Hymnal 1982.*

During the hymn, the deacon:

1. (Takes the key to the aumbry or tabernacle and) goes to the place where the sacrament is reserved.

2. Returns to the altar bearing the vessels containing the sacrament, places them on the corporal (toward the back), and genuflects or bows low.

3. Puts the paten on the corporal and places the consecrated bread on it. If the bread is a loaf, or a number of large wafers, breaks the bread into enough pieces for the intending communicants.

4. Puts the chalice(s) on the corporal and fills them.

i. When all is in readiness, or when the hymn is ended, the deacon begins the Lord's Prayer (with hands extended), first saying or singing, "Let us pray in the words our Savior Christ has taught us."

j. The breaking of the bread that usually follows the Lord's Prayer is omitted (BCP p. 408). The anthem that accompanies it ("Christ our Passover" or "Lamb of God") is therefore also omitted.

k. After the Lord's Prayer the deacon, holding a portion of the bread over the chalice with one hand, and lifting up the chalice with the other, says the invitation to communion, "The Gifts of God for the People of God."

l. The deacon then receives communion, communicates the lay eucharistic ministers, and, assisted by them, communicates the people. During communion, hymns, psalms, or anthems may be sung.

m. The service concludes in the usual way, except that the deacon does not give a blessing.

12

The Bishop at Parish Eucharists

The bishop's visitation is an important event in the life of a parish family. It is also an occasion when, because of changes in the Book of Common Prayer, the expectation of what is to take place has altered, too.

In order to be as helpful as possible, this book includes the full historic ceremonial of the bishop's eucharist. At the same time, recognizing that most of our churches are small, concrete ways of simplifying that ceremonial—to make it appropriate to the space and resources available in particular churches—are suggested.

1. Of the Bishop as Principal Celebrant

For centuries in the western church, people have thought of the bishop's visitation largely in terms of the administration of confirmation. So absolute was this connection that it was sometimes questioned whether there was any purpose in the bishop making the visit if there were no candidates to receive it.

This very narrow view of the bishop's liturgical office stands in marked contrast to that of the early and patristic periods, when the bishop was regarded as par eminence a sign of the church's unity in Christ. To the people of those periods, the church was seen primarily as an assembly of all the Christians in a given community, presided over by one bishop, assisted by the college of presbyters and the deacons, and gathered around one table at which they shared the one bread by which they were made one body (1 Cor. 10:17).

With the growth of the church, the ideal of a single assembly for worship in each city became increasingly difficult to maintain, and, with the spread of Christianity outside the larger cities, was necessarily abandoned. What was not abandoned, however, was the view of the bishop as one set apart for the "apostolic work of leading, supervising, and uniting the Church" (BCP p. 510).

Rather than greatly increasing the number of bishops (the result of which would have been to diminish the sense of unity even more), the solution adopted was to deputize presbyters to preside at the eucharist in the bishop's name. Seen from this perspective, when the bishop's eucharist is scheduled to take place in a parish church, the bishop is taking the opportunity to preside in person, rather than by deputy. It is precisely this view which accounts for the first rubric on page 354 of the present Prayer Book.

There are indications that in the early centuries bishops arranged to preside personally in what we would call parish churches. In some places, one such occasion was the patronal feast or the anniversary of the dedication of such churches. Another practice, attested from the fifth century, was for the bishop to preside at the larger "downtown" churches on selected Sundays and holy days. On other Sundays and holy days, and especially on the principal feasts and in Holy Week, the bishop's "station" was at the cathedral. The most ambitious scheme of all was the ancient practice of the church at Rome where, in addition to customs such as those just mentioned, there was a "stational" eucharist on the weekdays of Lent, at which the bishop presided at a different church each day.

It is important to note that these services did not include confirmation or baptism. Christian initiation ordinarily took place only on a few specified days in the year and only in the cathedral and (at a later time) a few selected "baptismal churches." The whole purpose of these "stational" liturgies was to allow the bishop, as chief priest and pastor, to preside in person at churches other than the cathedral.

Circumstances today are, of course, very different. The bishop's visitation will normally continue to include confirmation, but that is now balanced by the bishop's presidency at the eucharist and baptism as well. The Prayer Book's expectation, moreover, that the readings at principal services will usually be those of the day (see pp. 300 and 414) makes possible a broader exercise of the bishop's office of interpreting the gospel than has frequently been the case.

There is still, however, much to be said for occasions when the bishop is present simply to preside and preach, in the ancient fashion. In smaller dioceses, where it is possible to avoid administering baptism and confirmation in Lent (as is desirable), the bishop might visit some of the churches of the diocese on the Sundays and some of the weekdays of the season for this very purpose.

Palm Sunday is a traditional occasion for the bishop to preside at the liturgy in the cathedral. It is also a day when, because of the length and nature of the proper liturgy (as well as its proximity to the Easter Vigil), the administration of baptism and confirmation is best avoided. Bishops other than the diocesan might appropriately make themselves available to preside (though not necessarily to preach) in parishes that would enjoy having a bishop share in their celebration of this important day.

2. Of Ministers Attending the Bishop

Traditionally, it is deacons, rather than "chaplains," who attend the bishop. (For examples of the recovery of this practice, see the services for the investiture and seating of a bishop in the *Book of Occasional Services*.) Three deacons (in dalmatics) appropriately minister at the bishop's eucharist. The first performs the usual duties of carrying in the gospel book, reading the gospel, leading the prayers of the people, and assisting at the altar. In addition, this deacon, from a conveniently placed seat, serves as master of ceremonies. The second and third walk on either side of the bishop, but a little behind, during the processions in and out. At the chair they occupy places at the bishop's right and left. During the eucharistic prayer they stand behind the concelebrating presbyters. In the absence of sufficient deacons, the duties of the second and/or third may be performed by priests. If such priests are also to be concelebrants, they wear chasubles. If not, they may wear copes. If there is no deacon present, the duties of the first are divided in the usual manner (2.4). In addition to the adult acolyte who will hold the service book for the bishop (unless this is to be done by one of the deacons), two other lay attendants will ordinarily be needed: one to hold the mitre and one to hold the staff. They vest in alb or surplice, and walk immediately behind the bishop and deacons in the processions in and out. In the chancel they occupy places from which they can easily bring the mitre and staff to the bishop when they are needed. (Since the bishop invariably receives the staff in the left hand, it is more convenient if the staff bearer's place is to the bishop's left.)

When bringing the mitre and staff to the bishop, and when receiving them back, the bearers either approach the bishop directly or, if it is more convenient, hand them to (and receive them back from) the deacons.

3. Of the Presbyters Who Are Present

It is desirable that the priests of the parish, as members of the college of presbyters, assist in the celebration as concelebrants. In the absence of a deacon, one of them, after receiving the bishop's blessing, reads the gospel.

4. Of the Bishop's Chair

The bishop's chair, strictly speaking, is the cathedra in the cathedral church. There is no need, therefore, for a special chair in parish churches. Indeed, it was not until the late nineteenth century that such chairs appeared in Episcopal churches. At parish liturgies, the bishop properly occupies the chair which would otherwise be used by a priest presiding at the celebration.

5. Of the Bishop's Vesture

In the course of the past few decades, the typical "picture" of a bishop functioning at a parish liturgy has changed from that of a figure robed in rochet and (usually black) chimere to one arrayed in cope and mitre. While this change is certainly to be welcomed as reflecting a heightened sense of celebration, it did not come about as a result of a change in the church's understanding or view of the episcopal office. Indeed, it is fully in keeping with the view of the 1928 and previous Books of Common Prayer.

In that view, which is directly traceable to the medieval western church, the bishop visited parish churches primarily to preach and to confirm. If the visitation included a celebration of the eucharist, the normal expectation was that the bishop would preside "over" it, by which was meant that the bishop would occupy a chair near the altar and pronounce the absolution and blessing. The cope is, of course, proper vesture for a bishop functioning in this way.

Such a view is not, however, the view of the present Prayer Book, which—following the more ancient understanding of the episcopal office described above—sees the bishop as the primary minister of all the sacraments. When present in a parish church, therefore, the expectation is that the bishop will ordinarily preside "at" the eucharist, that is to say, will function as the principal celebrant, as well as being the preacher. The historic vesture for a bishop functioning in this way is chasuble and mitre.

In another recovery of older practice, the Prayer Book also provides for the incorporation of most of the other sacramental rites—baptism, confirmation, unction, marriage, ordination—into the framework of the eucharistic rite itself. Formerly, when this was the norm, it did not involve a change of vestments: the bishop wore the chasuble throughout. The recovery of this ancient practice is specifically recommended.

Where this recommendation is adopted, the bishop will use a cope only at services which do not include presiding at the celebration of the eucharist.

6. Of the Pastoral Staff

The pastoral staff is in origin a walking stick, to which the symbolism of a shepherd's crook was subsequently attached. In keeping with its function, it should be carried by the bishop personally—rather than being borne by someone else—and used as a walking stick. (It is important to distinguish the pastoral staff from a primatial or archiepiscopal cross, which is always borne by someone else.) Customarily, the bishop carries the staff in the left hand, with the crook facing outward.

When not in use, the staff is held by an attendant, with the crook facing the bearer, or put aside in a convenient place, but not on or against the altar. (For the only exception to this practice, see the rite for the recognition and investiture of a diocesan in the *Book of Occasional Services*.)

It must not be assumed, however, that the staff can simply be put aside in a corner. Many staffs are top-heavy and tend to fall down. A stand, hook, or wall bracket (such as those used for processional crosses) will usually be needed.

Originally, the staff was considered a part of the episcopal insignia, and was used by all bishops. An echo of this ancient understanding can be seen in the rubrics for the ordination of a bishop, which permit the delivery of a staff to all bishops on the occasion of their ordination (BCP p. 553).

In Anglican practice, however, the staff has more frequently been regarded as a symbol of jurisdiction, and its use, by right, restricted to diocesan bishops. Where this understanding is in force, coadjutor, suffragan, assistant, and other bishops use the staff only when officially representing the diocesan, and never in the diocesan's presence. Visiting bishops, when presiding at services in such dioceses, do not use the staff at all.

Roman practice since the Second Vatican Council is a modified form of the same understanding. The right to use the staff belongs to the diocesan alone, who may, and normally does, permit its use by any other bishop, including retired and visiting bishops, when officiating within the territorial boundaries of the diocese.

It is not a part of the purpose of this writer to enter into debate about the merits of these varying usages. At services in which the staff is not to be used, the references to it in the directions that follow should simply be passed over.

At the eucharist, the staff is used by the bishop while walking in procession, during the reading of the gospel, and while pronouncing the absolution and the blessing.

When more than one bishop is present, only the one who is the principal celebrant uses the staff. (The only exception is the investiture of a diocesan.)

7. Of Mitres

Only in recent times has it become common to design mitres to "match" specific sets of vestments. The older and more practical tradition was to design them to look well with vestments of various colors and designs.

The most ancient form of mitre was of plain white linen, sometimes decorated with white braid or piping ("white on white"). The only touch of color was that the ends of the lappets (the two narrow bands that hang down the back) were frequently dyed a deep red. Later in history, as more elaborate mitres appeared, this became known as the "plain" or "simple" mitre, and its use was largely restricted to penitential occasions. There is, however, no need to continue this restriction today. Such a mitre looks well with many contemporary vestments, and bishops who prefer simplicity in such matters may appropriately decide to use no other kind.

Of the later forms of mitre, the most practical is the "golden mitre," made of golden cloth or of white cloth decorated with gold. It is appropriately used by bishops on all except penitential occasions or, if preferred, may be used only on occasions of special festivity. It may be noted that at services at which more than one bishop is present and officiating (which will not often happen in parish churches), it is traditional that only the principal bishop-celebrant use the golden mitre; the others use the plain one.

The use made of the mitre can be simple or complex. The tendency today is toward simplicity; in the past it was frequently highly elaborate. Beneath the elaborations, however, certain general principles have remained constant, and may be summarized as follows:

The bishop wears the mitre:

a. When entering and leaving the church in procession, and when going in formal procession from one part of the church to another, such as from the altar to a font located some distance away.

b. When giving absolutions and blessings, and when pronouncing declarative formulas such as "I baptize you . . ." at baptism and "Receive this Bible . . ." at ordinations.

c. When seated.

The mitre is not worn:

a. During prayers, whether said by the bishop or led by someone else. (The only exception is litanies sung or said in procession.)

b. During the proclamation of the liturgical gospel.

c. At any point from the beginning of the eucharistic prayer until after the postcommunion prayer.

When not being used, the mitre is held by an attendant or laid aside by an attendant on a credence table or in some other convenient place (not, however, on the altar).

8. Of the Bishop's Stole or Pallium

Ancient portraits and mosaics show that fourth and fifth century bishops wore the stole over the chasuble in the following distinctive manner. It is first put on in the same way as a priest's stole, but with the right end allowed to hang lower. The part hanging from the right shoulder is then passed around the neck, over the left shoulder, and allowed to fall down the back. Finally, the part pressing against the throat is pulled down to the breast and, when necessary, pinned to the part of the stole hanging down the front. The effect is quite attractive, and serves well to distinguish bishops from presbyters. (Such a stole functions best if it can be seen clearly, which usually means that it needs to contrast significantly with the chasuble worn beneath it. It stays in place best if it is made of material that is not slippery.)

In the west, the stole worn in this manner developed into the white woolen pallium with black crosses bestowed by the Pope on archbishops and the bishops of certain historic sees. In the east, however, a stole (pallium) worn over the other vestments in the ancient manner continues as the distinctive vestment of the episcopate.

The first such usage in the west in modern times was at the consecration of a bishop for the Lusitanian Church of Portugal—which is now a part of the Anglican Communion—who preferred it to the use of a mitre. The practice is commended here, whether used in place of or in addition to a mitre.

9. Of the Pectoral Cross

The pectoral cross is worn over the alb and under the stole and chasuble.

10. Of the Bishop's Ring

The bishop's ring is worn on the index finger or on the "ring finger" of the right hand, as may be preferred.

11. Of Lights Carried Before the Bishop

In larger churches, when the diocesan (and no one else) presides, in place of the two lights that ordinarily accompany the cross, seven torches or candles may be carried. Two of the bearers walk on either side of the cross, the third and fourth walk immediately behind them, and the fifth, sixth, and seventh walk three abreast. If the way is narrow, two precede the cross, two follow it, the fifth walks alone, and the sixth and seventh walk together.

On arrival before the altar, the bearers divide into two groups, four going to the right, and three to the left, so that the bishop can pass between them. Then, when possible, the lights (or some of them) are put in convenient places within the chancel. Those that are not are taken out and extinguished.

Two of them are (lighted and) carried in the gospel procession, and all seven are used during the procession out.

12. Of the Liturgy Itself

The Holy Eucharist is celebrated as described in chapter 6, the "Synopsis of Ceremonies" (6.1–6.63), with the following exceptions. (For suggested ways of simplifying the ceremonial, see section 13 below.)

The bishop, as principal celebrant:

a. Vests in the sacristy in alb (with amice and cincture), pectoral cross, stole, chasuble, and mitre. May, following ancient precedent, wear a dalmatic (always white and preferably lightweight) under the chasuble.

b. If incense is used, puts some into the censer before the procession begins.

c. Receives the pastoral staff.

d. Attended by two deacons (when possible), enters the church in procession. Where it is desired or expected, blesses the people by continually making the sign of the cross with the right hand.

e. On arrival before the altar, gives up the staff and mitre. Then reverences the altar with a low bow (or genuflection) simultaneously with the deacons. Then, where it is the custom, kisses and/or censes the altar.

f. Proceeds without mitre and without staff, to the chair. (The service continues as described in 6.8–12.)

g. After the collect of the day, sits and puts on the mitre. Remains mitred during the reading of the lessons and the psalm.

h. If a hymn is sung after the second reading, may stand (still mitred) and join in the singing up to the point where the preparations for the gospel are to be made.

i. Sits, mitred, to put on incense (if it is to be used at the gospel) and to bless the deacon who will read it.

j. When the gospel procession sets out, takes off the mitre, hands it to a deacon or to the mitre bearer, and stands. Makes the usual crosses on the forehead, lips, and breast, and then takes the pastoral staff. Holds the staff and faces the reader during the reading of the gospel.

k. Gives up the staff and puts on the mitre, if it is to be worn while preaching, and proceeds to the place where the sermon is to be preached. (If not the preacher, gives up the staff, sits, and puts on the mitre.)

l. Stands, without mitre, during the recitation of the creed.

m. If the rector or deacon makes the announcements at this point, sits and is mitred. (This is also the appropriate place for the rector to welcome the bishop.)

n. Stands, without mitre, for the reading of the names and the prayers of the people. Says the collect at the end of the prayers.

o. If the confession of sin is used, joins in it, and then, before pronouncing the absolution, puts on the mitre and takes the staff. After the absolution, gives up the staff, but retains the mitre for the exchange of peace. If the confession is not used, puts on the mitre before beginning the exchange of peace.

p. Sits, mitred, while the table is prepared. (If a hymn is sung at this point, may stand and join in the singing.)

q. Takes off the mitre before going to the altar. (Continues the service as described in 6.32–52.)

r. After giving the invitation to communion, "The gifts of God for the People of God," receives communion at the hands of the rector of the parish or another concelebrant. (Continues the service as described in 6.55–57.)

s. Standing at the chair or at the altar, says "Let us pray" with hands joined; then leads the postcommunion prayer with hands extended.

t. If oil of chrism is needed for use at subsequent baptisms in the parish, consecrates it using the form provided in the *Book of Occasional Services*.

u. Puts on the mitre. Blesses the people using either a short or long form, or the form with versicles on page 523 of the Prayer Book. Just before the trinitarian blessing, takes the staff in the left hand. Makes the sign of the cross over the people three times while blessing them (first to the left, then directly ahead, and finally to the right). But in Lent, if a prayer over the people is used instead, says it with hands outstretched over the people, and does not put on the mitre and take the staff until after the dismissal.

v. Retains both mitre and staff during the concluding reverence to the altar and the procession out.

13. Of Simplified Ceremonial

In many instances, because of the traditions of particular parishes or dioceses, limitations of space in the chancel area, or a shortage of persons to assist, it will be found necessary to simplify the ceremonial described in the preceding section. In such circumstances, any of the following alternatives may appropriately be adopted.

a. The bishop may preside at the eucharist in the same manner as a priest, making no use of either staff or mitre. In such cases, the wearing of the stole in the manner described in section 8 above is particularly appropriate.

b. The bishop may use the mitre and staff only during the entrance procession (giving them up before reverencing the altar) and while giving the blessing at the end of the service (and retaining them for the final reverence and procession out).

When this alternative is used, the duties of taking the staff and mitre from the bishop at the end of the entrance procession, putting them in a suitable place, and then bringing them to the bishop for the final blessing, can be carried out by the deacons (when present) or by servers who may also be performing other duties in the course of the liturgy. If necessary, this can even be done by the candlebearers who, after putting their candlesticks or torches in their proper places, can proceed directly to the bishop to take the staff and mitre. (It should again be noted that neither mitre nor staff is appropriately placed on the altar.)

c. The bishop may omit the use of the mitre and make use of the staff only, not only at the entrance and at the blessing and departure, but (if desired) at the gospel and absolution as well.

d. The bishop may use only the mitre, wearing it during the entrance procession and at the blessing and departure.

In some dioceses it is not uncommon for bishops (both active and retired) to be called upon to act as "supply priests" in mission churches and vacant parishes. When performing this function, it is suggested that the bishop usually preside in the same manner as a priest. When the celebration takes place on a principal feast, however, or on an occasion of local importance, such as a patronal feast, it would be appropriate for the bishop to enhance the sense of festivity by making a simple use of the mitre and/or staff as suggested in alternatives "b," "c," and "d" above.

14. Of the Bishop at Celebrations by a Presbyter

When the bishop is present on occasions when it is deemed more appropriate that a presbyter should preside at the eucharistic action (such as a significant anniversary of a priest's ordination), either of the following alternatives may appropriately be chosen.

In both cases, the bishop:

a. Walks at the end of the procession.

b. Is accompanied by such attendants as are needed to assist with the staff and/or mitre.

The presbyter may preside throughout the rite, in which case a chair for the bishop is made ready at a convenient place, such as the north side of the chancel. Since there is no necessity for the bishop to kneel, a kneeling desk is not needed.

In the course of the service, the bishop:

a. Enters vested in rochet, chimere, and stole; or in alb or rochet, stole, cope, and mitre. If intending to function as a concelebrant, wears alb, stole, chasuble, and mitre. Uses the staff and mitre only during the entrance procession and at the blessing and departure.

b. If the confession is said, pronounces the absolution.

c. If concelebrating, approaches the altar just before the eucharistic prayer. If not, approaches it during the breaking of the bread. Immediately after the invitation to communion, communicates the priest and is communicated in turn.

d. Pronounces the blessing at the end of the service.

If it is more convenient, the bishop may, after communion, go to the chair behind the altar. Then, after the priest has led the postcommunion prayer from the altar and turned to face the bishop (the deacon and acolyte likewise turning), the bishop pronounces the blessing.

If incense is used at the service, it is the priest, not the bishop, who puts it in the censer (and blesses it).

(The preceding ceremonial is also appropriate for bishops of other jurisdictions, and retired bishops, who are present as invited preachers.)

Alternatively, the bishop may preside at the liturgy of the word, in which case:

a. The service is ordered as described above (12.12.a–p). If not intending to concelebrate, the bishop wears a cope instead of a chasuble.

b. The priest, in chasuble, walks immediately in front of the bishop in the entrance procession and, after reverencing (and kissing) the altar, goes to a convenient seat.

c. After the deacon has prepared the table, the priest bows to the bishop, goes to the altar (puts on incense and officiates at the incensation), washes the hands, says the great thanksgiving, and breaks the bread. Unless concelebrating, the bishop stays at the chair, standing, and without mitre. The deacon ministers at the altar in the usual way.

If there is no deacon or concelebrating presbyter present, the priest goes to the altar at the offertory.

d. At the invitation to communion, the bishop comes to the altar (if not already there), communicates the priest and is communicated in turn, then returns to the chair and sits.

e. The bishop leads the postcommunion prayer from the chair or from the altar; and then, mitred and holding the staff, pronounces the blessing.

13

The Bishop at Holy Baptism

1. Of Baptism at a Principal Eucharist

When the bishop presides at baptism within the eucharist at a principal service on a Sunday or other feast, the liturgical color and the proper are those of the day. For exceptions, see chapter 7, "The Holy Eucharist with Baptism."

In addition to the preparations listed above (7.1), the following are made ready:

a. A chair or faldstool, to be placed in front of the altar or at the entrance to the chancel after the sermon.

b. (Optionally) an extra amice, or a white cloth of about the same size and preferably thicker, folded. This cloth, known as a gremial, is spread over the bishop's lap during the anointing with chrism in order to protect the vestments.

c. If chrism is to be consecrated during the service, an ampulla or other vessel containing olive oil, to which a small amount of oil of balsam or other fragrant oil has previously been added, is placed on the table by the font.

2. Of the Service Itself

The service begins as described in "The Bishop at Parish Eucharists" (12.12), with the following exception:

In place of the collect for purity, the bishop says the appointed versicles with hands joined (BCP p. 299). Gloria in excelsis may follow.

After the sermon, the service continues as described in "The Holy Eucharist with Baptism" (7.3), with the following exceptions:

a. A chair or faldstool is placed before the altar or at the entrance to the chancel. The bishop goes to it and sits. The deacons (if present) stand at the bishop's right and left. The bearers of the staff and mitre stand nearby. (If a simpler ceremonial is desired, the bishop may use the mitre only during the parts of the baptismal rite listed in "b" below, and omit the use of the staff entirely.)

b. Seated, and wearing the mitre, and holding the staff in the left hand, the bishop presides at the presentation of the candidates (7.3.f), the renunciations, the presentation of other candidates (if any are present), the question addressed to the congregation, and the commitment to the baptismal covenant.

c. After the last question, the bishop rises, and if the petitions for the candidates are to be said during the procession, says the invitation to prayer, "Let us now pray for…."

d. Still mitred, and carrying the staff, the bishop goes in procession to the font (7.4.a), preceded by the presbyters who will baptize the candidates, and attended by the deacons and other attendants. The candidates for baptism and their sponsors follow. The other candidates remain at the front of the church.

e. On arrival at the font the bishop takes a position behind it, facing the people, gives up the staff, and removes the mitre. Then, if the invitation to prayer for the candidates was not said earlier, the bishop says it now. The deacon or a person appointed leads the petitions.

f. The bishop says the prayer that concludes the petitions, the Prayer Book or sacramentary being held by the acolyte or by a deacon.

g. Unless water is already running in the font, one of the candlebearers fills it with water or pours additional water into the font or pool.

h. The bishop says the thanksgiving over the water with the usual gestures (7.4.f).

i. If chrism is to be consecrated, a deacon or a server takes the vessel of oil and holds it before the bishop. The bishop places a hand upon it and says the appointed prayer.

j. The bishop puts on the mitre, then stands aside while the rector or other priests or deacons baptize the candidates, and during the clothing of the candidates and the presentation of candles (7.4.g–i).

k. During the procession to the chancel, the bishop carries the staff. If the bishop sprinkles the people (7.4.k), the vat of water is carried by a deacon or server at the bishop's right. If the bishop has consecrated chrism, a deacon or server carries the vessel during the procession.

l. On arrival at the chancel, the bishop goes to the chair or faldstool, gives up the staff, takes off the mitre, and stands facing the people. The candidates stand facing the bishop. The acolyte or a deacon holds the book for the bishop.

m. With hands outstretched, palms down, the bishop says the appointed prayer over the candidates.

n. The bishop then sits, puts on the mitre, and, if it is to be used, receives the gremial from a server and spreads it over the knees. But if the anointing is to be done using the first method suggested (7.4.p), the bishop may prefer to stand (and to transfer the episcopal ring to the other hand). In this case the gremial will not be needed, but the bishop does put on the mitre. If the second method is used, it is customary to sit. In either case, the deacon or server with the chrism stands at the bishop's side.

o. The candidates come before the bishop one by one, the adults and older children standing or kneeling, as the bishop may find more convenient. A sponsor may place a hand on each candidate's shoulder during the laying on of hands and anointing.

p. The bishop performs the laying on of hands and anointing. In each instance, the rector or someone else nearby first pronounces the person's name aloud.

q. After cleansing the hand used for the anointing (7.4.q), the bishop (removes the gremial and) stands, still wearing the mitre.

r. Invited by the bishop, all join in welcoming the newly baptized.

s. The newly baptized then extinguish their candles (except at the Easter Vigil).

t. Then, unless confirmation, reception, and/or the reaffirmation of vows is to follow, the bishop begins the exchange of the peace (7.4.t).

The bishop then returns to the chair behind the altar and the service continues with the announcements and prayers of the people.

3. Of Confirmation, Reception, and Reaffirmation

When these rites immediately follow baptism, the bishop omits the exchange of the peace and continues the service as follows:

a. Standing at the chair or faldstool, and without mitre, the bishop says to the congregation, "Let us now pray for *these persons* who *have* renewed *their* commitment to Christ."

b. A period of silent prayer follows.

c. Then the bishop, with hands outstretched, palms down, over the candidates, says the appointed prayer.

d. The candidates come before the bishop, one by one, and stand or kneel in accordance with local custom. The bishop, still standing, and without mitre, lays both hands upon the head of each, saying the formula appropriate to each one. (It is more convenient if the confirmands come forward first, then those to be received, and then those who have reaffirmed their vows.) In each instance, the rector, or someone else nearby, first pronounces the person's name aloud.

e. Alternatively, the candidates may stand or kneel in order before the bishop, who then goes to them for the laying on of hands.

f. When the rites for all the candidates have been completed, the bishop, facing them, and with hands extended, says the prayer, "Almighty and everliving God, let your fatherly hand . . ."

g. The bishop then puts on the mitre.

h. The peace follows, at which time the bishop kisses the newly baptized infants and exchanges the peace with the other newly baptized persons and those who have been confirmed, received, or who have reaffirmed their vows, before proceeding to exchange it with the clergy.

i. The bishop then returns to the chair behind the altar, and the service continues with the announcements and prayers of the people (7.4.u). It is especially appropriate that the newly baptized receive their first communion at the hands of the bishop and one of the deacons.

4. Of Confirmation, Reception, and Reaffirmation without Baptism

When the bishop presides at these rites within a principal eucharist on a Sunday or other feast, the liturgical color and the proper are those of the day.

Should none of the readings relate to the rites being celebrated, the bishop may, except on principal feasts, substitute one or more (one is generally sufficient) of those appointed at no. 11 on page 929 of the Prayer Book. The collect for confirmation may also be used.

When these rites are celebrated at a separate service on other than a principal feast, the collect, psalm, and readings are selected from those appointed for confirmation, and the color may be white or red. If the Holy Eucharist is not celebrated, a cope is worn in place of a chasuble.

The service begins as described in "The Bishop at Parish Eucharists" (12.12), with the following exception:

In place of the collect for purity, the bishop says the appointed versicles with hands joined (BCP p. 413). Gloria in excelsis may follow.

After the sermon, the service continues as follows:

a. A chair or faldstool is placed before the altar or at the entrance to the chancel. The bishop goes to it and sits. The deacons (if present) stand at the bishop's right and left. The bearers of the staff and mitre stand nearby.

b. Seated, and wearing the mitre (and, if desired, holding the staff), the bishop presides at the presentation and examination of the candidates, and the commitment to the baptismal covenant.

c. After the last question, the bishop (gives up the staff and) takes off the mitre, stands, and says, "Let us now pray for *these persons* who *have* renewed *their* commitment to Christ."

d. A period of silence follows.

e. The bishop then continues the service as described above (13.3.c–g).

f. The peace follows, at which time the bishop exchanges it with those who have been confirmed, received, or who have reaffirmed their vows, before proceeding to exchange it with the clergy.

g. The bishop then returns to the chair behind the altar, and the service continues with the announcements and the prayers of the people. At a principal service, the short form given in the appendix (15.3) may be used. At other services the prayers may be omitted.

The confession of sin is omitted.

Except on principal feasts, the proper preface of baptism or of Pentecost may be used.

It should be noted that the ceremonial suggested in this book for use at confirmation is not that prescribed in the Roman rite. In that rite, the outward sign is an anointing, and it is administered with a declarative formula. The bishop therefore sits with mitre on. In Anglican usage--which is based on an equally venerable ancient practice--the outward sign is a laying on of hands accompanied by prayer. For this kind of ceremony, the traditional posture is standing with head uncovered.

Since the laying on of hands has historically been associated with blessings of all kinds, it is recommended for use at reception and reaffirmation as well.

It may also be noted that the practice whereby, after confirming each candidate, the bishop touches the cheek of each one is not recommended. This gesture, borrowed from the pre-Vatican II Roman rite, has sometimes been understood as a "slap" or "gentle striking," and interpreted as a reminder of the need to endure hardship for Christ's sake. In origin, however, the gesture was a medieval substitute for the kiss of peace, as the words that accompanied it in Roman practice, "Pax tecum," continued to bear witness. (Anciently, it was customary for bishops to greet each candidate with the peace immediately after the laying on of hands.) Since the exchange of the peace has now been restored to our own rite--albeit at a slightly later point in the service--there would appear to be no reason to introduce or continue using this ceremony.

14

The Ordination of Priests and Deacons

The rites for the ordination of presbyters and deacons, which now frequently take place in parish churches as well as in cathedrals, follow an identical pattern up to the point of the ordination itself. The following directions apply to both rites.

The liturgical color is white or red. But if the ordination takes place at a principal service on a Sunday or major feast, the color is of the day. On such days, furthermore, one or more of the readings and the collect are also appropriately those of the day.

Before the service, a chair or faldstool for the bishop is placed before the altar or at the entrance to the chancel. To its right and left are placed seats for the deacons who will attend the bishop. Seating is also provided for the presbyters selected to concelebrate and for others to be accommodated in the chancel. If the candidate is to sit in the chancel during the readings and sermon, a seat is reserved for that purpose.

In a convenient place, a small table or portable lectern is placed (sideways to the congregation), having on it a copy of the declaration the candidate will sign, and a pen.

The stole and chasuble for the new priest, or the stole and dalmatic for the new deacon, are placed in readiness. White or festal vestments are always appropriate for the newly ordained, regardless of the color being worn by others.

The Bible to be presented to the newly ordained is placed on the credence or in some other convenient place (not on the altar).

If, at the ordination of a priest, a chalice and paten are to be presented, it is desirable that they be the ones that will be used at the service.

The ordinand vests in an alb (with amice and cincture).

In places where the mitre and staff are customarily used only at the beginning and end of the eucharistic rite, the bishop may elect to use them at only one point in the ordination service proper, namely, during the presentation of the candidate (items "b" through "e" below).

1. At the Ordination of a Priest or Deacon

The service begins as described in 12.12.

a. In the entrance procession, the candidate and presenters walk immediately ahead of the deacon with the gospel book, and after the deacons who will not be performing a liturgical function and the priests who will not be concelebrating. Incense may be used at the entrance, but the altar need not be censed, especially if the position of the bishop's chair makes it inconvenient.

b. After the collect for purity, the bishop sits and puts on the mitre (and may hold the staff with the left hand). The presenters and ordinand come forward, bow to the bishop, and the presentation is made.

c. At the appropriate point, the ordinand goes to the table or lectern provided, signs the declaration, and returns.

d. The bishop then stands (all likewise standing) and addresses the congregation in the appointed words.

e. After the questions, the bishop (gives up the staff and) takes off the mitre and calls the people to prayer. The presenters return to their places. The ordinand kneels in a convenient place or, if preferred, lies prostrate, head toward the altar. The litany follows, the bishop and others kneeling. The bishop uses the faldstool or chair as a kneeling desk. After the Kyries (which may be sung by the congregation or choir in threefold, sixfold, or ninefold form), the bishop stands and faces the people for the salutation and collect.

f. The ministry of the word takes place in the usual way, the first two lessons invariably being read by lay persons. After the sermon, the small table or lectern where the declaration was signed is removed from the chancel.

g. The bishop sits, wearing the mitre (and may hold the staff), during the examination of the candidate.

2. Of the Consecration of a Priest

a. The bishop (gives up the staff and) takes off the mitre and stands. The presbyters take their places at the bishop's right and left, leaving room for the acolyte or deacon who will hold the book for the bishop. The ordinand kneels facing the bishop. The appointed hymn and a period of silent prayer follow.

b. Standing without mitre, the bishop begins the prayer of consecration with hands extended, places them on the ordinand's head at the point indicated--the presbyters also laying on hands--then continues the prayer with hands extended. (If the number of priests present is large, it is suitable that only a few of them lay hands on the ordinand with the bishop, and that the others extend their right hands toward the ordinand.)

c. After the prayer, the bishop sits and puts on the mitre. The new priest stands and is vested, preferably by another priest. In the meantime, a deacon or server brings a Bible to the bishop. At the same time, if there is to be a presentation of vessels, a deacon or server goes to the credence, uncovers the vessels, takes the empty chalice and paten, and goes to the bishop's side.

d. The new priest then kneels before the bishop, who presents the Bible with the appointed words. The new priest then hands the Bible to the deacon or server who brought it, who puts it in a convenient place.

e. The bishop may then present the chalice and paten, either in silence or with the words, "Receive these vessels as a sign of the authority given you to preside at the celebration of the Holy Eucharist." The new priest then hands them to the deacon or server who brought them, who then places them on the altar.

f. The bishop stands, still wearing the mitre, and greets the new priest, who also stands.

g. The new priest then begins the exchange of the peace and is greeted by the other priests, and by others as convenient.

h. After the peace, the bishop and attendants proceed to the chair behind the altar. The seats in front of the altar are removed.

i. At the eucharist which follows, the new priest concelebrates with the bishop, joins in the breaking of the bread, gives communion to the bishop, receives communion from the bishop, may assist in communicating the people, (does not join in the postcommunion prayer,) and gives the blessing at the end of the service.

j. After the dismissal, the bishop puts on the mitre, receives the staff, and goes out in the usual way.

3. Of the Consecration of a Deacon

a. The bishop (gives up the staff and) takes off the mitre and stands. The ordinand kneels facing the bishop. The appointed hymn and a period of silent prayer follow. An acolyte or deacon holds the book in readiness for the bishop.

b. Standing without mitre, the bishop begins the prayer of consecration with hands extended, places them on the ordinand's head at the point indicated, then continues the prayer with hands extended.

c. After the prayer, the bishop sits and puts on the mitre. The new deacon stands and is vested, preferably by another deacon. In the meantime, a deacon or server brings a Bible to the bishop.

d. The new deacon then kneels before the bishop, who presents the Bible with the appointed words. The new deacon then stands and hands the Bible to the deacon or server who brought it, who puts it in a convenient place.

e. The bishop stands, still wearing the mitre, and begins the exchange of the peace. The bishop and clergy greet the new deacon, as do others as may be convenient.

f. After the peace, the bishop and attendants proceed to the chair behind the altar. The seats in front of the altar are removed.

g. At the eucharist that follows, the new deacon performs the functions assigned to the deacon in chapter six (nos. 29–56), stands at the bishop's right during the postcommunion prayer (but does not join in it), and says the dismissal. One of the other deacons present appropriately performs the functions described in nos. 57–58.

In the sacristy, following the service, the bishop signs the certificate of ordination, and presents it to the new priest or deacon.

4. Of More Than One Candidate

In some dioceses, because of the number of candidates, it is customary to ordain several deacons at the same service. Where this is the case, the following procedures are recommended:

a. At the time of consecration, the candidates kneel side by side, but far enough apart that they do not appear to be crowded together. The hymn and period of silent prayer take place as usual.

b. Standing without mitre, the bishop says the first paragraph of the prayer with hands extended. Then laying hands on the candidate in the center of the row, says the second paragraph. Then, moving from candidate to candidate, repeats the words, beginning, "Father, through Jesus Christ your Son," over each of the other candidates, while laying on hands (rubric, BCP p. 554). Finally, returning to the center, says the concluding paragraph with hands extended.

c. The bishop then sits and puts on the mitre. The new deacons stand and are vested, preferably by other deacons. In the meantime, deacons or servers bearing Bibles come to the bishop's side.

d. The new deacons approach the bishop one at a time, kneel, and are presented with a Bible as described in 3d above. The peace follows.

At the eucharist that follows, the diaconal duties are shared (rubric, BCP p. 554).

When priests are ordained, the requirement that the presbyters present join in the laying on of hands makes the ordination of multiple candidates more difficult to arrange. It is suggested that not more than two be ordained at the same service.

15

Appendix

Liturgical Texts

1. Psalms at the Rite of Baptism

Gloria Patri is not used with these psalms.

a. During the Procession to the Font

Refrain: As the deer longs for the water-brooks, so longs my soul for you, O God.

Psalm 42: Verses 2,3 / 4,5 / 6,7

b. During the Clothing of the Candidates

Refrain: As many of you as have been baptized into Christ have clothed yourselves with Christ.

Psalm 32: Verses 1,2 / 3,4 / 5,6 / 7,8 / 9,10 /11,12

Only as many pairs of verses as are needed are used.

c. During the Clothing or During the Procession to the Chancel

Refrain: The Lord is my shepherd; I shall not be in want.

Psalm 23: Verses 2,3 / 4ab,4cd / 5,6

or this:

Refrain: As many of you as have been baptized into Christ have clothed yourselves with Christ.

Psalm 23: Verses 1,2 / 3,4 / 5,6

2. Anthems During the Sprinkling of the Congregation

a. During Easter Season

I saw water proceeding out of the temple; from the right side it flowed, alleluia; and all those to whom that water came shall be saved, and shall say, alleluia, alleluia.

b. At Other Times

I will sprinkle clean water on you and you shall be clean; and a new spirit will I put within you, says the Lord.

3. Prayers of the People at Baptism or Confirmation

As appropriate, the second or third of the following petitions is omitted or adapted to the circumstances.

Deacon or other leader

In peace, let us pray to the Lord, saying, "Lord, have mercy."

For the holy Church of God in every place, and especially for this parish (*or* congregation) and diocese, and for *N.(N.)* our bishop(s), let us pray to the Lord.
Lord, have mercy.

For *those* (*or* "N.N.") baptized here today (*or* tonight), and for *those* who sponsored *them*, let us pray to the Lord.
Lord, have mercy.

For *those* (*or* "N.N.") who *have* been confirmed ("or" received into the communion of this Church) *[and]* (*those* who *have* renewed *their* vows), let us pray to the Lord.
Lord, have mercy.

For the welfare of the world, for this nation and its leaders, for this city (town, village, _____), and for every city and community, let us pray to the Lord.
Lord, have mercy.

For the sick, the suffering, the hungry, and the lonely; and those in any need or trouble, let us pray to the Lord.
Lord, have mercy.

For all who have died in the hope of the resurrection, and for all the departed, let us pray to the Lord.
Lord, have mercy.

In the communion of [the ever-blessed Virgin Mary, (*blessed N.*) and all the saints, let us commend ourselves, and one another, and all our life to Christ our God.
To you, O Lord our God.

Silence

The Celebrant adds a concluding Collect, such as Collect 6 or 16 in Lesser Feasts and Fasts (pp. 60 or 65), or the following Doxology:

For you anoint our head with oil and spread a table before us, and to you we give glory, Father, Son, and Holy Spirit, now and for ever. *Amen.*

4. The Setting Apart of Lustral Water

In the absence of baptismal water, the priest may set apart water for sprinkling the people, using this form. The blessing is said over the vessel of water, in the sacristy, at a convenient time before the service. A server or other person makes the responses.

Priest: The Lord be with you.
Answer: And also with you.

Priest: Let us give thanks to the Lord our God.
Answer: It is right to give him thanks and praise.

Priest: We thank you, Almighty God, for the gift of water. Over it the Holy Spirit moved in the beginning of creation. Through it you led the children of Israel out of their bondage in Egypt into the land of promise. In it your Son Jesus received the baptism of John and was anointed by the Holy Spirit as the Messiah, the Christ, to lead us, through his death and resurrection, from the bondage of sin into everlasting life.

We thank you, Father, for the water of Baptism. In it we are buried with Christ in his death. By it we share in his resurrection. Through it we are reborn by the Holy Spirit. Therefore in joyful obedience to your Son, we bring into his fellowship those who come to him in faith, baptizing them in the Name of the Father, and of the Son, and of the Holy Spirit.

At the following words, the Priest touches the water:

Grant by the power of your Holy Spirit, that those who are sprinkled with this water as a reminder of their Baptism may continue for ever in the risen life of Jesus Christ our Savior.

To him, to you, and to the Holy Spirit, be all honor and glory, now and for ever. *Amen.*

5. Communion Psalms

Refrains that include "Hallelujah" are not used in Lent.

a. Refrain: My God prepares a table before me.
   or   Receive the Body of Christ, taste the fountain of immortality. (Hallelujah!)
   or   Hallelujah, hallelujah, hallelujah!
  Psalm 23:   Verses 1 / 2 / 3 / 4 / 5 / 6

b. Refrain: Taste and see that the Lord is good.
   or   Taste and see that the Lord is good; happy are they who trust in him!
   or   Taste and see that the Lord is good; hallelujah, hallelujah, (hallelujah)!
  Psalm 34:   *Verses as selected by the cantor.*

c. Refrain: The eyes of all wait upon you, O Lord, and you give them
              their food in due season.
   Psalm 145: *Verses as selected by the cantor.*

d. Refrain: Hallelujah, hallelujah, hallelujah!
   Psalm 148: *Verses as selected by the cantor.*

e. Refrain: Hallelujah, hallelujah, hallelujah!
   Psalm 150: Verses 1 / 2 / 3 / 4 / 5 / 6

At the end of the Communion Psalm, the cantor may sing the Gloria Patri, after which the refrain is repeated for the last time.

The texts in this Appendix may be freely reproduced, especially for the purpose of providing musical settings.

16

Glossary

ablutions the rinsing of the communion vessels after communion.

affusion the practice of baptizing a person by pouring water on the head.

alb a white full-length tunic with narrow sleeves.

alleluia a song sung during the gospel procession, usually consisting of a verse of Scripture preceded and followed by "alleluia." (see also "tract")

altar book the large-print edition of the Holy Eucharist used by the priest-celebrant both at the chair and at the altar.

amice an oblong piece of white cloth, with tape ties, worn about the neck to conceal clothing worn underneath it and to protect the fabric of vestments.

ampulla a vessel designed to be poured from, used for the blessing, consecration, and administration of holy oils.

aumbry a small, usually ornate, cupboard built into or affixed to a wall, used for the safe-keeping of the reserved sacrament or the holy oils.

baptismal shell a shallow vessel used at baptism to pick up water from the font and pour it on the baptizand's head.

boat a vessel, shaped like a gravy boat, with a flanged cover, from which incense is spooned out into the censer.

burse a case for corporals, frequently richly embroidered.

cantor a person who sings the verses of the responsorial psalm, the verse of the alleluia, and other parts of the liturgy that are soloistic in nature but are not assigned to the priest or deacon.

cassock a close-fitting, usually black, garment that covers the entire body—originally the street wear of clergy—worn beneath a surplice or rochet, and sometimes beneath the alb. Bishops wear purple cassocks.

cathedra the chair in a cathedral church reserved for use by the bishop, and used by other bishops only at the diocesan's invitation.

censer a vessel for incense, consisting of a metal bowl suspended from a chain or chains, with a lid operated by a separate chain or a handle. Also called a thurible.

chalice the cup used to hold the wine at the eucharist.

chancel the part of a church, usually raised one or more steps, where the altar and seats for the clergy are located.

chasuble a vestment worn by bishops and priests, usually oval in shape, with a hole in the center for the head to pass through.

chimere a close-fitting black or scarlet garment, without sleeves, worn by bishops over the rochet.

chrism the oil used to anoint the newly baptized, consisting of olive oil mixed with oil of balsam or some other aromatic oil or oils.

ciborium a chalice-like vessel, with a cover, used to reserve the consecrated bread of the eucharist. Also called a standing pyx.

cincture a thick cord, preferably white, with knotted ends, used as a belt to secure or shorten an alb. Also called a girdle.

concelebration a eucharist at which other priests or bishops, vested according to their order, join the principal celebrant at the altar for the eucharistic prayer.

cope a cape-like festal garment, often of rich fabric, worn in liturgical processions and at non-eucharistic services. Historically, its use was not confined to clergy.

corporal a square of linen which is spread on the altar at the offertory, and on which the communion vessels are placed.

cotta a much abbreviated form of the surplice, sometimes worn by servers and choristers.

dalmatic a knee-length tunic with wide sleeves worn by deacons.

dominical words the words of Christ at the Last Supper: "This is my Body . . ." and "This is my Blood...." Also called the "words of institution."

doxology words of praise and glory to God. Used especially to refer to the concluding sentence of eucharistic prayers and to the Gloria Patri and its metrical equivalents, such as "Praise God, from whom all blessings flow."

elements the bread and wine of the eucharist.

faldstool a seat, shaped like a folding stool, with a cushion but no back, sometimes used by bishops when seated in front of the altar or at the chancel steps.

flagon a vessel for wine, larger than a cruet, usually with a handle and spout, and with a cover or stopper.

followers sleeve-like objects which are placed on the tops of candles to keep them from dripping.

font a large stone or metal bowl, supported by a pedestal, used to hold the water of baptism.

formulary a fixed liturgical text.

fraction the act of breaking the bread for communion.

frontal a cloth for the altar, usually of rich material, that hangs to the floor in front of it.

genuflection an act of reverence to the consecrated bread and wine, done by touching the right knee to the floor.

gradual a psalm or portion of a psalm, with a refrain, sung after the first reading at the eucharist. Also called a responsorial psalm.

gremial a white lap cloth or apron used by bishops to protect the vestments when performing anointings while seated.

lavabo the ceremonial rinsing of the celebrant's hands before the eucharistic prayer.

lectern a reading stand.

lectionary a table of appointed Scripture lessons (see BCP pp. 889-931) or a book containing the text of the lessons to be read.

lector a person appointed to read lessons at the liturgy.

litany a form of prayer, sung or read by a deacon or other leader, with fixed congregational responses.

liturgy literally, "work of the people." A term used to describe the church's worship in general and the Holy Eucharist in particular.

lustral water water set apart for sprinkling as a reminder of baptism. Popularly called "holy water."

maniple a ceremonial handkerchief, designed to match the other vestments, worn on the left forearm.

mitre the distinctive hat worn by bishops at liturgical services.

oblations the offerings of bread and wine.

offertory the act of receiving and presenting the people's offerings of bread and wine, and of money or other gifts.

oil stock a small cylindrical metal object, with a screw-on cover, packed with cotton soaked in holy oil. In anointing, the minister touches the cotton with the thumb, and with it traces a cross on the person's brow.

pall a square of cardboard or plastic, covered with linen, used to cover a chalice. The word is also used to describe the cloth covering placed on coffins at funerals.

paten the plate for bread used at the eucharist.

pectoral cross the cross worn on the breast by bishops.

presbyters literally, "elders." The New Testament term for the order of ministers commonly called "priests."

presidential chair the seat in a church reserved for the member of the clergy who presides at the liturgy.

pulpit fall a cloth, usually embroidered, that hangs from the reading desk of a pulpit.

purificator a napkin used to wipe the chalice.

pyx a small box, frequently shaped like a pocket watch and suspended from a cord worn about the neck, used to take the consecrated bread to those who are sick or shut in.

rochet a surplice-like, white garment with close sleeves worn by bishops (in place of an alb) under the chimere, and sometimes under a cope. Organists frequently wear sleeveless rochets.

rubrics directions for the conduct of services, originally (and sometimes still) printed in red.

sacramentary a book containing the priest's parts of sacramental rites, but not the parts—such as the lessons—that are to be read by others. The Episcopal Church's "altar book" is a partial sacramentary.

sequence a metrical hymn sung between the lessons at the eucharist.

species the bread and wine of the eucharist.

stole a long band of fabric, frequently embroidered or ornamented, worn in different ways by bishops and priests, and by deacons.

surplice a very full knee to ankle-length white garment (derived from the alb) gathered at the neck and with wide sleeves.

tabernacle a small safe, usually ornate, affixed to the top of an altar, shelf, or pedestal, used for the safe-keeping of the reserved sacrament.

thurible another name for a censer.

thurifer the person who handles the censer during services.

tract verses of a psalm, or a short psalm, sung without a refrain, used in place of an alleluia during Lent. (see also "alleluia")

vested a word used to describe persons wearing liturgical garments.

versicle a short verse, usually from Scripture, said or sung by one person, to which the congregation responds with an appropriate fixed response.